ARMENIAN
TRAGEDY

ARMENIAN TRAGEDY

by Yuri Rost

Translated by
ELIZABETH ROBERTS

ST. MARTIN'S PRESS, NEW YORK

Original text and photographs Copyright © by Yuri Rost, 1990
Translation Copyright © by Elizabeth Roberts, 1990
Maps by Richard Natkiel Associates

First published in the United States of America in 1990

Printed in Great Britain

ISBN 0–312–04611–1

Library of Congress Cataloging-in-Publication Data

Rost, Yuri.
    Armenian Tragedy/by Yuri Rost
        p.   cm.
    ISBN 0–312–04611–1
    1. Armenians—Azerbaijan S.S.R.—Nagorno-Karabakhskaĩa
avtonomnaĩa
oblast'—History—20th century.   2. Nagorno-Karabakhskaĩa
avtonomnaĩa oblast' (Azerbaijan S.S.R.)—Ethnic relations.
3. Earthquakes—Armenian S.S.R.   I. Title.
DK693.5.A75R67   1990
947'91—do20   89-70181
                                                   CIP

Contents

Illustrations

ARMENIAN TRAGEDY

Tanks stand guard in Lenin Square, Erevan.
Time-worn face of tragedy.
Yurts serving as medical stations in Dzhrashen.
The long wait begins – it will be many years before the people can
  rebuild their cities and their lives.

Foreword

It was in February 1988 that the world's attention was first drawn to Nagorny Karabakh, Armenia and Azerbaijan. By no means everything that happened was reported in the Moscow press; too much was kept secret or underwent tendentious distortion.

In this documentary book by the Soviet photojournalist Yuri Rost, an attempt has been made to give, as far as possible, a full, objective description of that tragic intercommunal conflict which has had such significance not only for the peoples of Transcaucasia but also for the USSR as a whole and for the fate of *perestroika*.

And at that very same time another great tragedy befell Armenia – the earthquake. Yuri Rost was at the scene of the disaster immediately after it happened and again three weeks later. It seems to me that, whilst Rost's account of his impressions is written with passion, the book is at the same time an accurate documentary record of considerable social and historical significance.

ANDREI SAKHAROV
June 1989

Author's Note

I do not wish the reader to think that I have taken upon myself the exceptional responsibility of apportioning blame on either of the two communities involved in the development of the serious conflict in Armenia and Azerbaijan. Both Armenia and Azerbaijan were put in a position where neither the state machine nor a flawed nationalities policy was capable of heading off the events described – one lie begets another. The lack of freedom which had long existed in the republics and adherence to the Soviet Union's policy of stifling a growing sense of national consciousness at whatever cost drew the two communities together on a collision course. But it was this conflict, with all its victims and however regrettable, that gave birth to the people's movement, which it is for the people themselves to consider and evaluate.

Which Armenian or Azerbaijani provoked this or that episode during the year the reader may judge for himself, but do not dismiss this account of events because it seems to concentrate mainly upon the struggle from the Armenian point of view, even in those cases where the actions were of a mutually savage character. I have described events as I saw them or as they were recounted to me, without preconceptions and trying to remain objective. Let another author describe this dramatic year in the life of the Azerbaijani people.

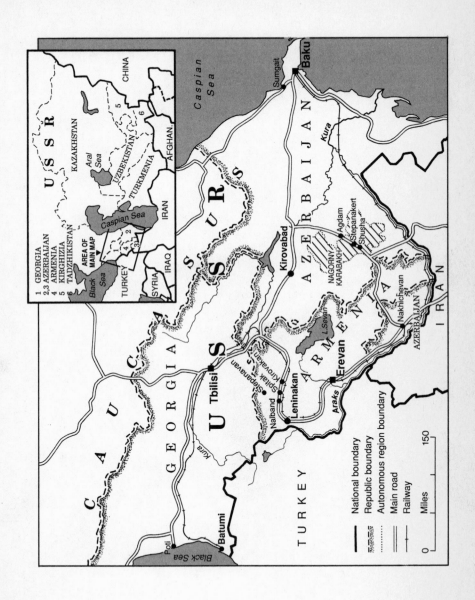

Inset map legend:

U S S R

CHINA

KAZAKHSTAN

Aral
Sea

UZBEKISTAN

TURKMENIA

AFGHAN.

Caspian Sea

IRAN

AREA OF
MAIN MAP

TURKEY

IRAQ

SYRIA

Black
Sea

1 GEORGIA
2,3 AZERBAIJAN
4 ARMENIA
5 KIRGHIZIA
6 TADZHIKISTAN

Main map labels:

Caspian Sea

Sumgait

Baku

Kura

AZERBAIJAN

Kirovabad

Agdam

Stepanakert

Shusha

NAGORNY
KARABAKH

L. Sevan

Nakhichevan

AZERBAIJAN

IRAN

U S S R

C A U C A S U S

GEORGIA

Tbilisi

Kirovakan

Stepanavan

Spitak

Nalband

Leninakan

ARMENIA

Erevan

Araks

Aras

TURKEY

Batumi

Poti

Black Sea

National boundary
Republic boundary
Autonomous region boundary
Main road
Railway

0   Miles   150

The Black Year of Awakening

On 7 December 1988 Olga Muradyan did not go to work. She told her employer that she felt unwell and asked for the day off. She had no temperature, aches or pains; her husband and children were well; nothing untoward had happened to her – life was peaceful, orderly and normal – but that morning she woke up with a feeling of apprehension and decided to stay at home. Her daughter went off to school, and her son, a second year student, to the polytechnic; her husband went to his building cooperative. Olga stood at the window and looked out from her fourth-floor flat over Leninakan.

The cathedral, only recently restored, had once towered over the whole city. Blocks over three storeys high had not been built for a long time following the earthquake of 1926. Though there were three- or four-storey blocks of flats in the town centre, most houses on the outskirts were single storey, made of the local tufa stone. In Khrushchev's time the five-storey, prefabricated concrete panel blocks had started to appear, cramped and uncomfortable. But they could be put up quickly and cheaply, and Leninakan was growing fast and there was a housing shortage. So these simple blocks were favoured by the architects even if they were concerned about their stability. It had been claimed that they would have a twenty-five-year lifespan, but they had already exceeded that and nobody was about to demolish them because prosperous Leninakan was still growing fast. Every year the population was increasing. People were leaving their villages and moving to regional centres, which were turning into small ugly replicas of bigger towns. From these regional capitals they then moved on into the bigger cities.

In Leninakan there had later sprung up a whole district of

nine-storey blocks of flats which were assumed, in the event of earthquakes, to be able to withstand shocks of up to 7 on the Soviet earthquake scale. These flats had bigger rooms and Olga often gazed over to these concrete towers: she must tell her husband, who was the boss of a building enterprise, to apply for a flat in one of the new blocks.

Olga looked up at the clock – it was twenty to twelve. Time was flying, it would soon be midday and she was still in her dressing gown – time to get going with the housework. But, instead, she stayed looking out of the window. Suddenly she felt she was about to die.

'Heart attack,' she said out loud, holding her left side. The floor was moving beneath her feet. She held on to the windowsill and saw the unfinished building opposite waving and collapsing.

'It's an earthquake!'

Olga ran out on to the landing amidst the thunder of collapsing walls and ran down the stairs. Ahead of her she saw her neighbour's son Armen Mestrolyan, who, with a shout of, 'Run for it,' was kicking at the door of a flat, trying to help the people inside escape.

The two of them ran together out of the collapsing building into the street. A neighbour who lived on the ground floor dashed up to them. Her face was contorted with fear.

'My daughter,' she screamed, 'Julietta! Armen – save her!'

Armen, without thinking, threw himself back into the building to the flat, seized the two-year-old child and managed to give her to her mother. At that moment, as a section of the house fell, burying Armen, his own mother ran into the courtyard.

'He's here, we saw him,' her neighbours reassured her.

In only forty-seven seconds the town was destroyed.

Olga, beside herself, rushed to the school and, seeing the mountain of smoking rubble, fell into a faint. When she came round, however, she opened her eyes to see her daughter's face looking down at her.

Afterwards, sitting in her brother-in-law's miraculously intact flat, she told me she had thought at that moment that she had died and gone to heaven. She could not believe that a single one of the pupils had escaped alive from the ruins of the school. But God had stretched out his hand over the family on that terrible day. The little girl had been sitting in class beside the door and at the first tremor had run out into the corridor. A concrete panel falling down from the wall had hit her from behind and sent her flying through a window, glass and all. She was left only scratched. A handful of the other children had also somehow survived; all the rest had perished. The earthquake had occurred four minutes before the bell for break. If it had happened only minutes later, a thousand children would have been saved, because in southern towns, even in winter, the children are allowed outside between every lesson.

The polytechnic institute, where Olga's son studied, was not completely flattened. At 11.40 Artur was walking down a corridor when suddenly right in front of him it was open to the sky. The walls ahead of him had collapsed. A few steps later and he would have been buried under a heap of concrete rubble. He remembers lying down as soon as he felt the earthquake.

Olga's husband Razmik came out of his reinforced concrete construction works and got into the car. Then it suddenly jumped off the ground. He opened the door to see what was happening to his Zhiguli car and heard the rumble of falling masonry.

This particular Armenian family was lucky – they survived. They were an exception. Maybe there are other families which remained intact, but I didn't meet any. More often I saw surviving fragments of families, old men left to fend for themselves, men and women prostrated by grief. . . . In less than an hour Armenia was shattered. Just like a stone thrown into water, the ripples of grief spread out in every direction and reached the hearts of millions in the USSR and beyond. The December earthquake was the bloody climax to a tragic year in the history of the Armenian people, a year of dramatic conflict, a year of awakening of national consciousness, a year of loss and struggle. A year when the two fateful place names Karabakh and Sumgait were branded on the hearts of Armenians.

Part I

CONFLICT

Territorial disputes are no longer a novelty, but in the USSR, after the creation of the Union, they had never been so intense, nor had they developed into a secret war between republics as has happened over the Nagorny Karabakh question. Democratization, which accompanied the *perestroika* announced by Mikhail Gorbachev, awakened feelings hitherto wholly or partially kept below the surface in the Soviet Union. Stalin's imperialist nationalities policy had once and for all, it seemed, assigned a place determined by the will of the central power to each national minority in the structure of the country. The borders limiting the territory of whole peoples were secured both by explicit and by secret legal acts. This happened basically in two periods: after the Civil War at the beginning of the 1920s, and after World War II. The same is true of the external borders of the state as a whole.

The internal borders which delineate the regional homelands of peoples were dictated by Stalin's will. The all-powerful Stalin would do anything, but even he could not move mountains, seas, towns and villages. He nevertheless managed to compensate for this minor disability through the forcible removal of whole peoples. The Crimean Tartars, Volga Germans, Chechens, Meskhetians and Ingushes were removed from their homelands and despatched to distant regions. Their historical homelands were settled by peoples that had not 'disgraced' themselves in the eyes of the Leader.

The rights of the original peoples to their own native lands were lost for ever, they were told. After Stalin's death, however, they gradually began to return to their own lands. Sometimes this process had a directed character, sometimes it was 'do-it-yourself'. Conflicts between the old and the new occupants were acute and sometimes bloody. The country as a whole, however, knew nothing whatever about them, due to control of the media and censorship. The Karabakh problem, against the background of other problems, cannot have seemed particularly acute to the authorities. More to the point, outside Azerbaijan, with its Nagorny Karabakh Autonomous Region, and outside Armenia, which aspired to reunification with the Azerbaijani enclave, the citizens of the USSR lived in total ignorance of the seething of nationalistic passions aroused by this question.

The Azerbaijani singer Rashid Beybukov used to sing in Azerbaijani a provocative song:

> 'With my jaunty Caucasian cap aslant,
> I'm the jolly lad from Karabakh and
> That's what they call me everywhere
> As my stallion's hooves ring on the air.'

The song implies that Karabakh is part of Azerbaijan, but in Karabakh they thought differently. It is not very big in area, but it is quite rich in natural resources. In 1923 the region was occupied 94.4% by Armenians and was separated from Armenia by a narrow strip of land about ten kilometres wide. Armenians had lived in Karabakh for a long time: cathedrals, castles, grave memorials bear witness to the many centuries of their settlement of these lands.

Only at the beginning of the 18th century did incoming non-Armenian ethnic masses from Central and Asia Minor and Kurdistan begin to affect the political situation in Nagorny Karabakh. Since that time, there has arisen in Karabakh not only a complex political, but also a complex religious situation. Although the Christian Armenians learned to live alongside the incoming Muslims, this co-existence was not without problems.

In April 1920, after the establishment of the Soviet regime in Azerbaijan, the President of the Revkom (Revolutionary Committee), N. Narimanov, demanded the annexation of Nagorny Karabakh, Nakhichevan and Zangezur to Azerbaijan. Stalin supported Narimanov: 'My opinion is that above all we must protect one of our flanks, in this case that of Azerbaijan with Turkey.'

However, the Party Central Committee took a different view. On 24 July 1920 Lenin wrote to Chicherin, his Commissar for Foreign Affairs, 'Shouldn't you make peace with Narimanov?' Chicherin replied stating: 'Karabakh has been an Armenian settlement since time immemorial.'

As a stop-gap measure, the Central Committee decided not to give the disputed territory to one or the other. Chicherin in conversation with Ordzhonikidze, the party boss in Transcaucasia, explained the Central Committee's line: 'You must insist that the disputed territory between Armenia and Azerbaijan should be occupied not by Azerbaijanis, but by Russian troops. Questions concerning the ownership of these territories will be postponed until a more favourable political climate is achieved.' This was due to the fact that Azerbaijan was under Soviet rule, whereas Armenia was not.

The day after the establishment of Soviet power in Armenia the disputed regions were transferred to Armenia: 'From this day [30 November 1920] the previous borders between Armenia and Azerbaijan are declared null and void. Nagorny Karabakh, Zanzegur and Nakhichevan are recognized as forming part of the Armenian Socialist Republic. [Signed:] The President of the Revolutionary Committee of Azerbaijan, N. Narimanov.'

After this declaration, some Bolsheviks thought the quarrel had been resolved. Ordzhonikidze in a speech on 1 December 1920 in Baku declared: 'Soviet power is capable of resolving all those wretched problems connected with interracial enmity, of which there are many in the world, including here: Zangezur, Nakhichevan and Karabakh. These places are the seat of the so-called Armenian–Muslim problem here in Transcaucasia, a problem which has led to horrors.' Ordzhonikidze had in mind the massacre of 1915 inflicted by the Turks on the Armenians, the folk memory of which lived on in subsequent generations of Armenians so that the word 'genocide'* in the USSR came to be associated largely with that event.

*In April 1915 the Turkish Government embarked on a policy of liquidation of its subject Armenian population. 1·5 million were shot in 1915–16. A further 1 million escaped to Europe (including Russia), the Middle East and America.

9

On 12 June 1921 Armenia announced that the previously disputed regions were now an irremovable part of the fabric of their republic. But the triumph of the Armenians was not long-lived – it lasted just three weeks.

As early as 5 July 1921, at the request of the same Narimanov, 'arising from the need for national peace between Muslims and Armenians', the office of Caucasian Affairs of the Party Central Committee in Moscow handed over the Karabakh region to Azerbaijan.

Later, in the course of the reorganization of the region, Karabakh lost its common border with Armenia and it became an island within Azerbaijan, although to this day three-quarters of the population consist of Armenians. Conditions of life on this Armenian island were fairly complex, if one wished to maintain contact with the motherland. The absence of television programmes in Armenian and colleges of further education, a shortage of schools, the obstacles to a business or a political career forced Karabakh Armenians, among them many artists, writers and poets, to leave their homeland. Living standards in the area were lower than the average in Azerbaijan or Armenia – all these factors together with memories of the massacre of Armenians in Shusha, the former capital of Karabakh, strengthened the persistent yearning of the Karabakh Armenians to be reunited with Armenia. However, this did not suit the Azerbaijanis living then and now within the disputed region. As far as the Azerbaijani Republic was concerned, it did not wish to hear of any handover of Karabakh to Armenia. All these passions were kept bottled up for a long time and only boiled over when people felt that *perestroika* and *glasnost* were no longer just trendy phrases.

During 1987 signatures for a petition were collected in Karabakh and local meetings were arranged in workplaces, at which people passed resolutions to put before the Soviet and Republic Governments calling for the transfer of Karabakh to Armenia.

These were not the first such expressions of popular opinion in modern times. In 1965, 50,000 signatures on a petition were collected from the total population of Karabakh of only 150,000. On that occasion the only copy of the petition was sent to Brezhnev. The question was not resolved, but many of those who had signed were deported from Karabakh. At the same time, books were published in Armenia about Karabakh and *samizdat* articles were printed, but until very recently there was no coordinated action.

In 1987 a campaign was once more launched to collect signatures, but this time the organizers were more astute. The petition, containing 82,000 signatures with forenames, surnames and addresses, was photocopied on the quiet and made into ten volumes, entitled *The Unification of Karabakh with Armenia*.

Simultaneously demonstrations were held, the first of which was on Saturday 18 September. The Armenian writer and journalist Zori Balayan, one of the leaders of the Karabakh movement at that time, told me about it later. He was both a witness to and a participant in many of the events described.

'Who was the organizer of the first demonstration?'

'Many people contributed, but without doubt the leader was Igor Muradyan, a rather serious chap, although he's only thirty-two.'

'What is his background?'

'He's an economist, a doctor of sciences.'

'A good speaker?'

'He can handle an audience all right. He's tall, good looking, but he stutters and hardly speaks any Armenian. He was born in Baku [the capital of Azerbaijan] and lived there for twenty-six years, then he moved to Armenia. He's a sophisticated intellectual. You might fault him on creative literature, but in political science and the politics of Armenia, he's brilliant. Added to that, he's fantastically persistent. Throughout his six years in Armenia he organized meetings with Moscow Armenians, and wrote letters to the central Government. He collected material on Gaidar Aliev. At that time, Aliev was a member of the Politburo of the Central Committee of the Communist Party of the USSR, the first secretary of the Communist Party of Azerbaijan and later the deputy president of the Council of Ministers. The material provided evidence of Gaidar Aliev's criminal activity and Igor sent it to the Prosecutor General of the USSR, who simply sent the documents back.

Then Igor sent the dossier to the President of the Supreme Court. When it was returned, he did not let the matter rest, but sent it back to Moscow, this time to the President of the Supreme Soviet of the USSR, Andrei Gromyko. Throughout all this he was constantly phoning and sending telegrams asking when the wrongdoer would be brought to justice. All this put him at risk of being put away for "psychiatric treatment", but he still persisted.'

'What happened at the meeting he organized?'

'It was more of a demonstration. People came out on to Bagramyan Prospect in Erevan with portraits of Gorbachev and slogans about *perestroika* like "Freedom for Karabakh" – reasonable, not extremist ones. The police seemed unprepared for an unauthorized public procession and sought to avoid confrontation. They pleaded with us: "What are you youngsters up to? Do you know where it could all end?"'

1988 began with the arrival in Moscow of a delegation from Karabakh. The delegates brought petitions for the unification of the area with Armenia and the ten volumes of *The Unification of Karabakh with Armenia*, and gave all the documents to Demichev, the Vice-President of the USSR. Demichev was impressed by all the work that had gone into them and promised to bring them to the attention of the Politburo. It was as if the Government did not fully appreciate how serious the situation was.

All of January and the beginning of February were spent collecting more signatures and holding small meetings, although their hopes were on Moscow to resolve the problem. But in Moscow, as usual, they procrastinated, assuming that the rift would somehow heal if a salve were applied. The salve was to consist of improvements in work and living conditions for the inhabitants of Karabakh.

In Baku the authorities did not anticipate the scale of the approaching disturbances, or perhaps they were simply ignorant of what was going on in Stepanakert, the capital of Karabakh. Once they realised, they sent V. Konovalov, the secretary of the Central Committee of the Communist Party of Azerbaijan, to the region.

At a gathering of local Party activists he called those who had taken part in the collection of signatures extremists and hooligans. He also took himself off for talks 'with Moscow', where, according to him, he was assured that the question of the unification of Karabakh and Armenia was not going to be reopened.

The following day the local Party bosses in Karabakh toured the area to calm people down. In the district of Gadrutsk, Osipov, the President of the Regional Executive Committee, ordered the collection of signatures to stop. In reply to this extraordinary demand, people gathered at the district Party committee offices and asked to be told what had been said at the party activists' meeting, warning that the question of Karabakh had to be decided without more ado. Osipov and the district Party secretaries asked them to disperse at once. However, nobody budged, the crowd stood there all night debating and in the morning demanded that the seal of the District Soviet of People's Deputies be affixed to the declaration which bore several thousand signatures. The deputies of the district soviet met, and their executive committee endorsed the declaration – an unheard of move in Soviet experience.

The following day local leaders were summoned to the regional headquarters of the Party, where they appeared in front of a group of officials from the Central Committee of the Communist Party of Azerbaijan. The journalist Nikolai Andreyev recalls what was said as follows:

First Official: 'The Central Committee of the Communist Party of the Soviet Union is aware of the disturbances in the Autonomous Region of Nagorny Karabakh and demands a stop to them. The Central Committee promises that the social and economic problems of the region will be resolved. But the territorial questions will not be reviewed. However, you, instead of calming people down and explaining to them the impossibility of this, sit in your offices and do nothing.'
Second Official: 'You have to talk with them bluntly. For example, you yourself, personally ... [he points at the district party secretary, V. Safaryan.] I am asking you: do you want Nagorny Karabakh to be united with Armenia?'

Safaryan hesitates to answer.

Third Official: 'Of course he does! You can see he does.'

Second Official: (to Safaryan) 'Are you a Communist?'

Third Official: 'In general, do you support the Soviet system or are you against it?'

Safaryan tries to say something, but is inaudible.

Second Official: 'They've all got to answer. Let's expose the real face of the nationalists.'

Safaryan (at last): 'Please advise us what we should do in this particular, concrete situation to normalize things.'

Kevorkov, first secretary of the Regional Committee of the Party: 'Nobody asked you to speak. Hold your tongue and listen to what you're told.'

L. Saakyan, a teacher and a deputy of the Supreme Soviet of the Azerbaijan Republic: 'Why are you being so rude? I must ask you to talk to us more politely.'

Safaryan: 'Will you tell us straight: are they going to reconsider the question about unification?'

Third Official: 'Listen to him! He's still going on about that. Think what will happen to you if the Azerbaijanis in the neighbourhood come to your village.'

Sarafyan: 'Is that a threat?'

Second Official: 'It's a piece of good advice. You live in a blind alley. Just think about it. Who's going to answer for the consequences?'

First Official: 'In any case, it's quite clear what's got to be done. They've lost control. It's beyond them, so we'll have to use the militia and break up these meetings. We'll fix the Prosecutor's office, and get them to pinpoint and punish the ringleaders as an example. Then the rest will shut up.'

The Party was relying on intimidating the public, but people were no longer afraid.

The seal which had been attached to the foot of the people's declaration on 12 February convinced everyone that justice could be achieved. Within a few days, during which there were endless meetings, the people won a sitting of the Karabakh Regional

Soviet because the expression of the people's will required legal formalization.

In Stepanakert, on 20 February, the Soviet voted to take Karabakh out of Azerbaijani jurisdiction and unite it with Armenia. This decision was backed by the trade unions and the Komsomol. And that was not all: a 40,000 strong crowd remained in the square day and night. Speakers one after another addressed them without a break.

A video film of these meetings shows women, men, children and old people. Above the crowds were portraits of Lenin, Gorbachev and Shaumyan (formerly Lenin's Special Commissar for Caucasian Affairs), and banners declaring 'Justice will prevail', 'One people – one territory' and 'The Karabakh question should be decided by Karabakh people'.

'Were you there at the time in Karabakh?' I asked Zori Balayan. 'You are from there, after all.'

'No, on 20 February I flew back from America. Coming down the aircraft steps I heard: "Karabakh, Karabakh". I immediately guessed that they had made the stupid mistake of asking for Karabakh to be made part of Armenia.'

'But didn't you yourself want that to happen?'

'Politics is the art of the possible and, after all, what does one mean by part of a part. Three hundred years ago we became part of the Russian empire. That empire became part of the Soviet Union. Problems of "enclaves" shouldn't exist, especially since borders within the whole country are arbitrary. The arguments should only be about who comes under what politically.'

'Within Azerbaijan?'

'No, within the Soviet Union as a whole, what happened in the end. I'm talking now about the creation under the central government of a special Karabakh control commission in January 1989. Down in Karabakh, they went about it the wrong way with their talk of redrawing frontiers, their extremism, their nationalism ... I remonstrated with them, promised to speak to the meeting to explain that the instigators of that session of the

Karabakh Regional Soviet had spoilt everything, but it was too late – the horse had bolted.'

TASS, the telegraph agency of the USSR, gave news of the unrest in Karabakh, and this led to a wave of meetings in Stepanakert and Erevan, the Armenian capital, where on Theatre Square half a million people gathered. There were strikes. In Stepanakert too they downed tools. *Pravda* and *Izvestiya* printed articles in which they branded everyone involved as extremists. *Pravda*'s own correspondent in Armenia dissociated himself from the article which went out under his by-line. The newspaper was burned in the streets.

High party officials arrived in Armenia and Azerbaijan: the secretary of the Central Committee of the Communist Party of the Soviet Union and the Vice-President of the USSR. During the night of 22–23 February the first secretary of the Karabakh Regional Party Committee was replaced. Now the area was being run by Pogosyan, who was fairly popular with the people. Meetings in Erevan attracted up to 700,000 people without a single incident of hooliganism. There were no troops in Erevan. The only element of disruption was that many workplaces were closed.

In Azerbaijan the tension was also rising, but for the time being everything was orderly. The newspapers in both republics were full of official articles about friendship and brotherhood between peoples.

In an area neighbouring Karabakh, at the Azerbaijani district centre of Agdam, a meeting was held on 21 February to discuss the resolution of the Karabakh Regional Soviet to unify with Armenia. Having discussed it, the audience dispersed.

Next day, on 22 February, several hundred young Azerbaijanis from Agdam set off for Askeran, an Armenian settlement in order, they explained as they left, 'to watch the demonstrations there'. As they approached Askeran two Azerbaijanis died. The circumstances of their deaths and even how they were killed remain a mystery, but, following word of their deaths, 20,000 people gathered and set off for Askeran threatening to 'teach them a lesson'.

The outcome of this march would have been unthinkable if it had actually reached Askeran, but fortunately local Party workers, mullahs and community leaders such as Khuraman Abbasova managed to halt the inflamed mob. The situation thus remained under control for the time being.

In the Azerbaijan capital of Baku everyone refused to consider even for a moment that Karabakh might be handed over to Armenia. After the session in Stepanakert, throughout Azerbaijan there swept a wave of meetings whose basic content was the endorsement of the Party's national policy and slogans such as 'Not an inch', 'Don't give an inch' and 'We won't give up a single square centimetre'. Requests from Stepanakert for unification with Armenia were seen as nibbling away at the territorial integrity of Azerbaijan. In this rare instance the people and the Party were indeed, as a slogan said, as one. In any case, the constitution of the USSR gave the Azerbaijanis grounds to be certain of their own case, for Article 78 proclaims: 'The territory of the Union's republics cannot be changed without their consent.'

On 24 February at a meeting of party activists in Baku, a textile worker from the Karabakh silk works, a member of the inspectorate of the Communist Party of Azerbaijan, gave a speech in which she tried to explain what was happening in Stepanakert, what the people there wanted. She was shouted down. 'Nationalist! Provocateur! Get out of the chamber. Get out of the Party.'

Meanwhile, the situation on the borders of the Karabakh region was becoming more tense. It was impossible to get to Stepanakert by road due to road blocks. Cars with Karabakh number plates were being stopped, passengers and drivers murdered, and their cars reduced to scrap metal.

At the frontier between Armenia and Azerbaijan the *Pravda* correspondent's car was stopped. Several members of the Lachin militia were patrolling the road.

'Documents please. Get out. You can't go any further.'

'I represent the newspaper of the Central Committee of the Communist Party of the Soviet Union. You will answer for this outrage.'

'You'll be the one to answer for it. Into the lockup!'

Freed the following day, he heard that the oil store at Askeran had just been ransacked; a mill had been attacked, in the course of which some grain had been destroyed; a cane processing works had been set alight; and many hectares of vineyards had been ruined.

In Stepanakert each such event was relayed to the crowds in the main square, arousing waves of hostile emotion. Emotion and that is all, for everyone was conscious that only self-control, discipline and the maintenance of order would save everyone in the enclave from catastrophic conflict.

It was becoming dangerous to cross the border into Azerbaijan proper. 'My husband is Armenian and works as a driver,' Tamara K. told me. 'On the 22nd of February he didn't go to work. He said there was a strike. I asked him, "Is that possible? Isn't that illegal?" That's what I said to him then. "You're working for a state factory." He respects me. He agreed and went to Agdam. On the way he was stopped and badly beaten up. When he got home he was a terrible sight. Our son said he would pay them back. But that would only have led to worse trouble.'

In Stepanakert and in the villages vigilante groups were formed to patrol the roads and streets at night. Hunting rifles were taken out of their boxes. Nevertheless, fewer than the normal number of offences were committed in the following six weeks.

It is curious to note that it was at precisely this time that two railtruck loads of vodka arrived in Stepanakert, although before the disturbances there had been no spirits whatever in town. The workers thought that this delivery of alcohol was a provocation and refused to unload the trucks.

The Soviet mass media preferred not to get involved in the interracial conflict, awaiting a signal and guidance on the way to cover the Karabakh situation. It was clear that a signal was imminent and the shape of the guidelines became quite transparent when TASS news agency made the following announcement:

24 February. A meeting of Party activists of the republic took place today in Baku to discuss the urgent need to improve the worsening situation in the Nagorny Karabakh Autonomous Region. Speeches have been made recently there appealing for the unification of Nagorny Karabakh with the territory of the Armenian SSR. Irresponsible extremist elements have been provoking breaches of public order.

Who these 'extremists' were, what proportion of the population they represented, what they wanted, what breaches of public order – all that was left unclear, but the general drift could be easily read. And many newspapers jostled to be ahead of the game, whipping up their readers with their own letters containing declarations such as:

Such events pierce our hearts . . . .
Nothing can mar the glowing feelings of friendship between our peoples. . . .
The Soviet peoples are one family – and this is what our Motherland always prided itself on. . . .
Beloved Armenian and Azerbaijani brothers! Time to get really down to work. Don't let us or yourselves down, brothers! Time comrades, to think clearly and get down to some serious work. At the end of the day, this is our international duty. . . .

The phrase 'international duty' had been associated for nine years with the war in Afghanistan, where, through stupid political mistakes and in the name of justifying dishonest slogans, simple Soviet and Afghan lads had died one after another, guilty of nothing whatever themselves. The false justification of the necessity of troops in Afghanistan was formulated precisely as 'international duty'.

This phrase was also evident in the letters published by newspapers about the Karabakh conflict. Readers used the phrase, apparently unaware of its nuance. The popular press created an image of Armenian 'extremists' and 'hooligan elements', stirring up their readers. The Armenian people as a whole was somehow above suspicion, although the Armenians were 'being led by a group of loudmouths'.

Meanwhile, two leading figures in the Armenian democratic movement, the poetess Silva Kaputikyan and my author friend Zori Balayan, were in Moscow, where they obtained an interview with Mikhail Gorbachev on 26 February.

'You are not bound to silence about your interview in the Kremlin?' I asked Balayan.

'No, that point didn't come up in our conversation.'

'How did the meeting go?'

'We were in Gorbachev's office for more than an hour. On our side there was Silva and me. On their side Gorbachev and Politburo member and Central Committee secretary Alexander Yakovlev. I started things off by saying that essentially the movement had achieved its aim, because it was important for us to get a hearing. Our cry had gone into the void all these years.'

'How did Gorbachev react to that?'

'I can't tell you exactly what was said or even the order in which things were discussed, because I wasn't taking notes and I was nervous. However, it was clear to me that the General Secretary was well briefed. He said that the previous day the Politburo had discussed the Karabakh problem for four hours and that he himself had studied the documents relating to the dispute for several days. Also, Silva and I told him of our personal ties with the disputed region. My father was People's Commissar for Education, and one of the reasons why he died in 1937 was Karabakh. The Ministry of Education transferred 200 Armenian schools in Karabakh to Azerbaijan, where they didn't even know the Armenian alphabet. Even under the Tsars things weren't as bad as that. I told him how we restored national monuments which were then vandalised in an attempt to falsify history.'

'How did Gorbachev react?'

'He listened attentively and then said to Silva, "Raisa Maksimovna and I both learned your poems by heart in the 1950s." Silva remarked that this was at a time of renaissance (bearing in mind that this must have been during the early years of Krushchev's regime, the de-throning of Stalin, the lifting of the Iron

Curtain). Gorbachev smiled and said, "I'll take you up on that: let's make a renaissance in Karabakh. I give you my word." Silva begged him to send a commission. He replied, "Why should you want a commission if the Politburo is looking after the problem? Commissions in our country only muddle things up. We understand perfectly well that there's a problem. Let's put out the fire." This meant that we were being invited to go to Erevan and damp things down. "There are 700,000 people standing in the square," I said, "we cannot skirt round the serious problems when we talk to these people." We were already walking towards the door. Gorbachev said, "Put out the fire without worrying about the windows." Which meant, say whatever you like, but remember that we are Communists and are not going to beat about the bush.'

'Next day, 27 February, we were back in Erevan. Silva went to tape an interview for the local television station, while I went to address a meeting.'

'Who called it?'

'Nobody, people just knew that we'd been with Gorbachev and were waiting to hear what we had to tell them about our visit. In Theatre Square and in nearby streets there were about half a million people standing waiting. I went to the microphone and said everything I could about Aliev, everything I could about Turkey, about the schools in Karabakh and about our discussion with Gorbachev. I said that the Secretariat of the Communist Party of the Central Committee of the USSR was charged with wrestling with this most painful problem. Then I suggested I should write a letter to General Secretary Gorbachev explaining that we were going back to work and would call off the strike.'

The events that Balayan was describing took place at 6 p.m. on 27 February. The bloody events in Sumgait had already begun, but in Erevan no one knew of this until 1 March. For the time being hundreds of hands were raised in agreement, two raised fingers in a V sign.

'Why do you raise your hands like that?' Zori asked the crowd. 'That isn't our sign. Ours is five fingers, standing for the five continents where Aremenians are to be found. But we're united – you must close those fingers into a fist, that's our sign.' And I saw 700,000 hands clench. I wept.' Zori, as he recounted this, wept again.

Then, right there in front of the crowd Zori Balayan sat and composed the text of a letter to Gorbachev. The enormous throng waited silently with portraits of Gorbachev in their hands.

Then Balayan came forward and said, 'Now, I want you either to crucify me or put your trust in me. We've already won a great victory. We can't prolong these meetings. We all need a rest to see how things develop further, to give the Government time to come to a decision. Agreed?'

The crowd raised their clenched fists, half a million of them.

'We must disperse. People at the back, turn around first and go home.'

At this point Igor Muradyan, who has already been mentioned, told them that there would be another meeting in Theatre Square on 26 March.

'Why specifically 26 March?' asked Balayan.

'I d-don't know,' replied Muradyan, stammering as usual, 'but they'll be back, rest assured.'

Muradyan was absolutely certain. The crowd had belonged to him unswervingly since the moment on 21 February when an Armenian Party functionary had made a dreary sermon of a speech to the crowd, followed at the microphone by the stutterer who did not even speak Armenian properly.

'Well, what of it? A member of the Central Committee spoke to you in his native tongue? What did he tell you? Nothing. I may be speaking in Russian, but I'm speaking of our common grief.'

From that moment on he became the unquestioned leader and, perhaps, in naming 26 March as the day for the next gathering, he wrested from Balayan the right to dominate the crowd. Afterwards everyone tried to guess why he had chosen that particular date.

As 26 March approached troops came into Erevan, journalists arrived, and Government decrees were prepared. Everyone was waiting to see what would happen and why that date had been chosen.

'He can't simply have said it off the top of his head,' I remarked to Balayan.

Then he pointed out that 23 March was the seventieth anniversary of the Armenian massacre in the Karabakh town of Shusha, so maybe Muradyan had got the date muddled. The outside world was already focusing on the later date. 'People rang up from various countries abroad asking what is going to happen on 26 March. But we ourselves didn't know the answer.

'How did he manage to attract such an enormous crowd?'

'It was a chain reaction. The first big meeting followed the decision of the Karabakh Executive Committee to be united with Armenia. It was spontaneous. Perhaps there was some sort of behind-the-scenes organization, but basically a crowd of that size can only gather of its own accord. And then after that Muradyan announced meetings and people came of their own accord – academics, workers, artists and thieves – a complete cross-section.'

'After the announcement of the meeting on the 26th, did all other meetings peter out?'

'No. Igor said the following day that he invited people chosen at workplaces and in collectives to come to the hall of the Writers Union to organize what was to become the Karabakh Committee. It didn't seem a very wise step to me. *Glasnost* and the freedom he sensed in the previous few days went to Muradyan's head. And it's true, there was something unprecedented going on: unsanctioned meetings of half a million people, strikes, demonstrations. . . .'

'Do you think he made a mistake advertising the meeting at the Writers Union?'

'No, I don't. It allowed people to understand that from among them – who had all been equal until that moment – there were certain "chosen ones". Before that everything was literally out in the open, in the square. After this, the leaders were going to inform those in the square what had been decided.'

On 28 February in Erevan, as before, nothing was yet known about Sumgait. In a tense atmosphere engendered by the struggle for its leadership, the Karabakh Committee was born. In the event, Igor Muradyan was elected chairman unopposed.

On 1 March, Zori Balayan, Silva Kaputikyan (neither of whom was on the Karabakh Committee) and Igor Muradyan were invited to the Central Committee of the Armenian Communist Party for talks. Also taking part were Dolgikh and Lukyanov, both secretaries of the Central Committee CPSU, and Trushin, the First Deputy Minister of Internal Affairs of the USSR.

Dolgikh, a candidate member of the Politburo, spoke first: 'Well, comrades, it's happened, just as Gorbachev feared it would – blood has been spilt, pillage and rape.'

That is how Erevan came to know about Sumgait, but even highly placed bureaucrats did not have details of the carnage. It was at this meeting that the word 'murder' was first mentioned. Dolgikh said that 12–14 people 'of various nationalities' had died.

'Something must be done,' he declared firmly.

'There is one way,' replied Igor Muradyan. 'You must accept that Sumgait was deliberate, that this is a reply to the peaceful demonstrations in Erevan. We knew that pogroms were possible before this happened. Only the extrication of Karabakh from Azerbaijani control can save the situation.'

'That's easy enough to say,' said Dolgikh.

'Are you a Communist?' Lukyanov asked Muradyan.

'No, I'm not.'

'I see. Well, well.'

Lukyanov, sitting opposite Balayan, seemed to him to be giving him a dirty look.

'Why are you looking at me in that hostile way? Is it just because I want my homeland Karabakh to be free?' asked Balayan angrily.

'I'm sorry,' said Lukyanov quietly. 'I can't help looking this way.'

'I felt terribly embarrassed,' Balayan told me afterwards. 'It was only later I noticed he had something wrong with his eyes. As a doctor I wanted the earth to swallow me up for my tactlessness. We apologised to each other. His courteous behaviour put me at an embarrassing disadvantage.'

Lukyanov went on: 'We've got to find a way to put an end to all this.'

But Silva Kaputikyan replied, 'We suggested the way to end it the other day, when we calmed the people down after our meeting with Gorbachev. We sent the crowd away from the square back to their workplaces. We reacted in a peaceful and understanding way to the General Secretary's statement of 26 February reported by TASS. The Azerbaijanis reaction was Sumgait. Are they now expecting us to smooth over the situation yet again?'

'It wasn't you that cooled the situation,' the officials replied, indicating how unimportant a part they thought had been played by the three protestors.

Meanwhile the country had come to hear scanty reports and rumours of the tragedy at Sumgait. A few days after the riots *Izvestiya* reported:

On 28 February in Sumgait disorderly scenes were provoked by a group of hooligan elements. Taking part in these illegal acts were people easily led, worthless and immature, who had fallen under the influence of false rumours concerning events in Nagorny Karabakh and Armenia. Criminal elements carried out rape and theft. 31 people died at their hands. Among them were people of various nationalities, old people and women. Decisive measures have been taken to normalize the situation. Those who committed these acts have been arrested and will answer to the full severity of Soviet law. The working people of the town showed restraint, demonstrating their sympathy with internationalism. The normal rhythm of work has not been disrupted.

The information in the above may be nil, but its implications are manifold. The earlier TASS communiqué and *Izvestiya* report together imply that the riots were provoked by Armenians, because mention had been made of extremists in *their* ranks. Furthermore, the aggression was apparently mutual, since people of 'various nationalities' had died.

'How can I tell you so that you'll understand? A few days ago I had everything – a husband, a son, a family, a house, a job, a car. We were a hard-working family.... They killed my husband, they killed Artur, my son.... I was saved by an Azerbaijani woman, a neighbour.' Fenya Avakyan covered her face with her hands. 'There in Karabakh, they are asking for unification. What have we in Sumgait got to do with it? Why do we Armenians have to be killed?'

Fenya was lying in a narrow room in the dispensary of a Sumgait factory. Beside her stood her sons Ashot and Aram. Their father was to have celebrated his sixtieth birthday on 27 February, but on that very day, the second day of the pogrom, Azerbajainis killed him and his son Artur.

Ashot, shocked and dazed, spoke slowly: 'My feelings for the Azerbaijanis? I'm ashamed for them. Not hatred. Revenge? On whom? Our neighbour? He has seven children.'

How did such atrocities come about? On 26 February Azerbaijani refugees from Armenia began arriving at Sumgait bus station, telling hair-raising stories of the indignities they had allegedly suffered. By the evening of their arrival newspaper kiosks and other small Armenian businesses were being put to the torch.

On 27 February tens of thousands of Azerbaijanis had gathered outside the offices of the Sumgait town soviet. From the rostrum refugees from Armenia demanded: 'Brothers, how can you forgive the disgrace and humiliation of our Azerbaijani women, our wives and daughters?'

The crowd screamed for vengeance: 'Throw the Armenians out of Sumgait!'

Attempts were made to calm the crowd. A mother-heroine* tried to speak, but she was shouted down. The famous poet Bakhtiar Bagab-Zade stepped on to the platform, but was hauled off. In vain a historian tried to explain the situation. At the microphone V. Guseinov, the director of the republic's Institute

*A decoration (with three classes) introduced in July 1944 to promote population growth following losses in World War II.

of Political Education, said: 'Karabakh was, is and will remain ours.'

'Hurrah!' replied the crowd.

'But this is no way to go about things. You do not represent the whole people. I am in possession of the facts. Hardly anything the refugees have told you here today is true.'

The crowd howled him down with insults.

It is difficult for a normal person to explain the behaviour of Muslim-Zade, first secretary of the Sumgait town soviet. He was on leave and only with the greatest of difficulty was he finally persuaded to cut short his holiday and return to town.

He told me later: 'Since my childhood I have worshipped the actions of that heroic rifleman Alexander Matrosov, who threw himself into the embrasure of an enemy pillbox and was posthumously decorated a Hero of the Soviet Union in 1943. And when I came to the noisy square, when I saw the crowd, then I knew that my hour had come.'

He climbed on to the platform and began to speak. The crowd didn't recognize him.

'Who are you then?' they cried.

'I am the first secretary of the town soviet.'

'Are you for us or against us?'

'I am for you.'

'Then why are you up there and not down here?'

Muslim-Zade climbed off the platform and reappeared at the front of the crowd moving off towards the Armenian quarter. The town became completely possessed by anti-Armenian fever. At first, the crowd restricted itself to burning cars and smashing shop windows. Then, suddenly, the situation exploded.

'I was on the street and I couldn't understand at the time why aggression turned in an instant into unbridled violence,' recalled Colonel Nofel Kerimov, the new commander of the Sumgait militia.

Later the reason became apparent. At that moment an announcement was made on the republic's television station about the two Azerbaijanis killed on 22 February in the Agdam region and that there were no casualties among the Armenian population.

No explanation was given of who had killed the Azerbaijanis with what weapons or under what circumstances. It is difficult to understand why, five days after the event, it was thought necessary to report these deaths, but it is hard to think of a more powerful detonator.

Arno Avakyan was killed right on his own front doorstep. His son Artur jumped out of the flat's first-floor window, but he didn't get far.... The killers knew which flats in the block were occupied by Armenians. Anyone on the street suspected of being Armenian was stopped and had his passport checked. Armed with metal bars, the mob beat, raped and killed. They broke into flats and totally destroyed the contents; any Armenians they came across were beaten to death. Furniture and books were piled in the yard by members of the mob and set alight.

'Our flat,' recalled Ashot Avakyan, 'looked as though an atom bomb had hit it.'

Cars were overturned and burned. The mob stoned and broke up first-aid minibuses that were trying to get the injured to hospital. Even the arrival of unarmed troops did not deter the rioters: the mob simply overturned the armoured personnel carriers and beat up the soldiers with iron bars. There was a complete breakdown of law and order in Sumgait lasting three days.

My descriptions of the events in Sumgait come from transcripts of evidence submitted to the Soviet High Court. But first, before quoting from them, I would like to quote from a book written in Tsarist times by Ambassador Nelidov entitled *Genocide of Armenians in the Ottoman Empire*:

From various Turkish quarters crowds of cut-throats emerged, armed with knives and staves with which they fell upon all those they took for Armenians, and thus started a series of most barbarous attacks on the defenceless and wholly innocent Christians. The police not only stood idly by witnessing the outrages as they occurred, but in many cases also took part in the killing and looting. The troops, who arrived far too late on the scene, also did nothing to stop them.

It has been officially established that, in 1988, in Sumgait the militia did not try to prevent lawless deeds, but even released some of the criminals who had been arrested by the troops on the street. The main bloody events took place in district 41a. The mob had lists of the Armenians living there. To quote again from Ambassador Nelidov's book: 'According to a carefully planned system, the bands of cut-throats were armed with knives, firearms, kerosene, and lead-tipped staves all of the same design.' Our newspapers reported that the killers in Sumgait were armed with knives, axes, firearms, sharpened metal poles all made in a similar way, and broken bottles, just as Nelidor said they had decades earlier in Constantinople.

Ambassador Nelidov again: '... Their leader, Khadzhi Bego, showed particular ferocity. He had a woman quartered and the parts were carried through the city for all to see. By the order of this same brute another woman was stripped and led through the streets of the village naked.'

All the rapes in Sumgait were gang rapes. The victims were humiliated in the entrances to teahouses and paraded through the yards and streets naked. Here is part of the summing-up of the prosecution case against the Sumgait murderers:

Led by A.I. Akhmedov, the group of hooligans who included, along-side other unknown persons, Ya.G. Dzhafarov and I.A. Izmailov, armed with staves, knives, metal bars, axes, stones and other objects, broke into flats where Armenian citizens were living, demolished doors, furniture and other articles of domestic equipment, smashed crockery and window-panes, threw the belongings out of the flats, set fire to them and looted. In 17 flats in district 41a their actions during the pogrom caused damage amounting to 215,919 roubles.

Akhmad Akhmedov was not a professional killer. He and the other two good-for-nothings had been to school, served in the army and then worked for local firms. None of them had been in court before.

On 29 February, at 2 p.m., Akhmedov came out of the gate of the spinning mill where he was employed as a senior press operator and set off home. At the junction of Peace and Friendship

Streets by the bus station he stopped to join in a meeting. The speakers said that in Nagorny Karabakh they were killing Azerbaijanis and raping their women. Somebody said that at Baladzhary station there was a coachload of corpses from Karabakh. All this led him to take part in the riot. When the call went up from the crowd to take revenge on Armenians, he snatched the megaphone from someone else and suggested that they all go to district 41a to ransack the Armenian flats there. The majority of the young men fell in with his suggestion and the mob moved off.

He had been quietly on his way home from work, but suddenly here he was urging through the microphone: 'Sack the Armenians' flats. Don't take their things, destroy them. Death to the Armenians. Muslims, destroy the Armenian flats. Armenians out. You don't know what is happening to our brothers and sisters in Nagorny Karabakh. What we are doing is a mere trifle by comparison. Muslims, destroy the Armenians, we'll kill them. Long live Azerbaijan. Brothers, they are killing our brothers and sisters in Karabakh, they'll kill you too.'

The court found Akhmedov, Dzhafarov and Izmailov guilty of killing the Melkumyan family, Arthash Aransiyan and Misha Ambartsumyan. At a separate hearing the court was told of further crimes committed by the same accused men. Akhmedov had joined up with Dzhafarov, Ismailov and others and begun to beat up another man called Arakelyan. During the course of the attack, Arakelyan was struck on the spine with an axe. Dzhafarov and Ismailov both then went for Arakelyan with hatchets, striking several blows each about his head and body. After his murder, the rioters set fire to his body. Arakelyan's wife was next. Dzhafarov, who had a knife, struck her several times in various parts of her body. Thinking her dead, since she showed no signs of life, he threw a mattress over her, poured inflammable liquid over it and set it alight, as a result of which Mrs Arakelyan died from terminal second- and third-degree burns to her shoulders and back.

Dzhafarov was formally charged that, with deliberate intent to kill and from hooligan impulse, he aimed a blow with an axe to the head of Edward Melkumyan, who was then thrown by others on to a fire burning near by.

It is almost impossible to believe that the events described took place towards the end of the twentieth century, but they did. Corroborative evidence from witnesses confirms that the events described actually did take place. A witness, E. Salamov, gave his version of how the Melkumyan family died: 'I saw that around entrance No. 3 to block 26, where Armenians lived, they were beating up a woman. She was a large, well set-up woman. I knew she was the mother of two Armenians boys. From entrance No. 3 they dragged a man of about thirty ... When they had dragged him out, they began to hit him. Then they took him away to the wooden walkway outside block 5v and started to beat him again. After that a man of between twenty-three and twenty-eight years old went over to him as he lay on the ground and threw a burning rag over his chest. The man jumped up screaming and ran round the back of block 26. I didn't see the man again. Later, I saw them dragging Irina from the second doorway of block 26. I knew her. The mob dragged her to the transformer hut. What they did to her I did not see. When the crowd dispersed, I saw that she was lying naked on the ground and a youth of about fourteen or fifteen was hitting her on the back with a spade. He struck her on the back full force about five or six times. Irina lifted herself up, waving her arms. He hit her again. Irina fell back. My father called me into our block. I don't know what time it was, but it was already getting dark, but I could see that Irina was dead. She was lying still with her eyes open and full of blood. She was in a sitting position, her back was against a wooden plank which was burning. There was nobody near her any more.'

It is bad enough to write about and to read these things, but not to know is even worse. Whole generations of Soviet people were brought up in ignorance of the brutal pages of their history. In ignorance and total social passivity we lost about 30 million people, annihilated by Stalinism, which was protected by the law of silence. If we wish to become a civilized society – which will not be easy, judging by what has been described above – we must learn to talk openly about all the horrors which are our heritage from Stalin.

What happened in Sumgait, notwithstanding that the court described the actions of the guilty men as evil hooliganism, was very like genocide. The crimes were massive. Extracts from the court record of the prosecution's case confirms this:

'Hundreds of citizens, basically of Azerbaijani nationality, took part in the accomplishment of these crimes. The pogroms of the flats, burning, beating, rape and killing were carried out by groups of degenerate hooligans. The part played by some of them was subsequently confirmed and carries criminal penalties ...'

'He was surrounded by fifteen to twenty men and they started to attack him with axes, knives and bars. They hit him about the body and the head. Then one of them pulled over a burning mattress and smothered the man with it ...' (Witness: D. Zerbaliev.)

'They stripped the girl and threw her into the refuse bin. Screaming, the girl tried to struggle free. Then a youth of twenty or twenty-two came up with a white teapot with little flowers on it. There was petrol in the teapot. He poured petrol over the girl and set light to her himself.' (Witness: M. Mamedov.)

'The top part of one man's body was on the bonfire, but his legs were sticking out. He was still showing signs of life, trying to get out of the fire, but some fellow was holding him down with an iron bar so he couldn't get out.' (Witness: M. Mamedov, accused of another serious criminal offence.)

'Two men dragged the prone man to the bonfire and threw him into the flames. Then youths came up and poked at his body with sticks.' (Witness: S. Erikeev.)

'I did not see anyone pour the petrol over him, but suddenly the upper part of his body burst into flames. He fell to the ground immediately and rolled about trying to put the flames out, but very soon was still.' (Witness: I. Baikov.)

Noisy demonstrations and meetings might have been expected in Erevan, but there were none – the people kept their word. But in

Stepanakert the square came to life once more in the middle of March. 40,000 Karabakh people stood before the regional committee offices and as one raised their left hands and cried, 'Plenum, plenum.' That night, all entrances to the town were blocked by lorries and makeshift barriers barred the streets. People in overcoats warmed themselves at bonfires next to the barriers. A car would draw up. Several people would go up to it from the bonfire to inspect the driver's documents. The driver would not object. The boot would be opened. This routine went on until 18 March, until the plenum of the Party Regional Committee.

Meanwhile, in Moscow, a delegation from Karabakh had secured a meeting with high officials to remind them of a potential troublespot. The delegates saw Vorotnikov, the Chairman of the Council of Ministers of the RSFSR, President Gromyko and finally Ligachev who, in Gorbachev's absence abroad on an official visit, felt himself to be running the whole country. It was at this moment that the newspaper *Soviet Russia* published an article by Nina Andreeva of Leningrad headlined 'I cannot give up my principles'. This was a neo-Stalinist manifesto, which took the country back to the old days of the 'shining future', to the Iron Curtain, to the hunting down of 'cosmopolitans' (Jews), to the stifling of any nascent signs of democratic freedom. Such an article could not have appeared without the sanction of a man who enjoyed high Party power. Ligachev was such a man. That this manifesto in a newspaper was, in essence, an attempted political putsch is also confirmed by the active way in which study groups were simultaneously set up in various regions by regional committees of the Party, which then published endorsements of the article. Many Party organizations received orders to discuss and support this attempt to revive a longing for a strong leader and a totalitarian regime.

Ligachev received a delegation of women teachers and explained to them that the question was being fermented by the intelligentsia, whilst the people were quietly getting on with their lives. He gave the impression that the basic problem which had to be grappled with was social rather than political.

On 18 March the plenum of Nagorny Karabakh Regional Committee, which the crowd in the square had demanded, was held.

It is interesting to note that, whereas previously the first secretary on the Regional Committee of the Party had always been an Armenian and the second secretary a Russian, on this particular occasion the Russian in question came from Baku, from the Azerbaijan Central Committee of the Party. It transpired that in Moscow the previous day Malkov, an official of the Central Committee CPSU, had been summoned by Razumovsky, the Central Committee secretary, and told that he must fly to Karabakh to take over as second secretary.

'When should I leave?'

'Now. At once'.

He left wearing what he stood up in, without seeing his wife or daughter, without any of his things. He had to get to the plenum – and he made it.

The crowd filled the square, blocking all approach roads. The new first secretary, Pogosyan, who was then unpopular, came out of the Regional Committee building and got into his car. As he did so, women held on to his trousers, mauled him and cried: 'Go back in and hold the plenum, then you can go home. We are going to occupy the printing works, so as to be sure that the decisions taken to unify us with Armenia are published. As soon as the newspaper is out, you can go home.'

Late at night in Stepanakert I was standing near the Regional Committee office building which was guarded by young pink-cheeked lads wearing helmets and flak jackets under greatcoats, carrying truncheons and with automatic weapons slung over their shoulders. These militiamen were peaceably inclined, but they were minutely inspecting passes to enter the building. One sergeant was from Kiev, another from Kharkov.

'Hard work?' I asked.

'Not now. There are lots of troops here. Tanks, armoured cars.'

'How about in February and March?'

'We weren't here then.'

A man without a pass came up and said, 'In March the Regional Committee was protected by the people, not by the militia. They only came later. In the spring we had democracy and we lived and breathed democracy. We were happy, we tasted freedom. You haven't a clue what it was like, because you didn't experience it and you never will. You destroyed it for us.' He said this in a friendly way, offered them Armenian cigarettes and went off into the darkness.

'A troublemaker,' said the sergeant without rancour.

'Who is he?'

'We've known him since way back. He's an ordinary bloke, only obsessed like they all are with this reunification business. "*Miatsum*' they call it in their language. They like to rabbit on about it.'

From the darkness the man emerged once more. 'But your lot voted for extracting Karabakh from the territory of Azerbaijan, too,' he said. 'When Malkov flew in from Moscow they brought him straight here in a car. The crowds parted to make way for him. "Here comes the new Russian," they said. So he passed through them, with only what he stood up in and a pack of cigarettes in his pocket. His wife sent his suitcase on later after him.'

'And what were the crowd shouting?'

'Nothing untoward. That he should vote at the plenum for the unification of Nagorny Karabakh with Armenia.'

'And so how did he vote?'

'In favour. Afterwards they asked him: "Tell us, could you have voted against" "I would have been a lunatic," he said. "Tell us honestly, did they give you instructions in Moscow to vote in favour? If not, then that vote really is something – you have slipped your leash haven't you?" Malkov said, "I would have been a fine one. The plenum elects me second secretary and a member of the bureau, and within an hour there is a vote, and I vote against? They would have had my guts for garters." He would not have come to any harm,' continued the man, 'but the reaction of the people on the square and at the plenum so affected him that he even tried to be one of the first to raise his hand to vote for the transfer of Nagorny Karabakh to Armenia.'

The plenum had begun at 8 a.m. 40,000 people waited for the

plenum to complete its work; not a single person left the square. From time to time the crowd chanted: 'Lenin. The Party. Gorbachev. *Miatsum. Aiyastan* [Armenia]', all of which was clearly audible within the council chamber. At 1.30 a.m., fifteen and a half hours later, the plenum meeting ended. The people in the square were awaiting its decision and the following text was read out to them:

> Expressing the aspirations of the Armenian inhabitants of the autonomous region and the will of the majority of the Communists of Nagorny Karabakh to ask the Politburo of the Central Committee of the CPSU to consider and answer positively the question of the unification of NK Autonomous Region with the Armenian SSR, thereby rectifying the historical mistake of the territorial allocation of Nagorny Karabakh.

People in the square hugged each other, cried with happiness shouted, 'Hurrah, *Miatsum.*' Nobody wanted to leave. They sang, made speeches, recited poems and eventually, towards dawn, the procession moved off to the printing works where the newspaper *Sovietsky Karabakh* was to publish the decision of the plenum.

The decision of the regional soviet, ie representatives of the local people sometimes called 'soviet power', had been made a month before; now the Party had taken its decision too. The people celebrated their victory.

Karabakh began to fill up with more VIPs than they had ever dreamed of. However, the situation was putting official circles in Moscow, Baku and Erevan on their guard. They had noted the activities of unofficial political societies, which had had a significant effect on public opinion. In Armenia the society was called simply 'Karabakh' and headed by Igor Muradyan; while in Nagorny Karabakh it was known as 'Krunk' (*Krunk* is Armenian for 'crane'; the bird is a symbol of homesickness). The society was motivated by historic patriotism and had set itself the aim of joining Karabakh to Armenia. When discontent arose in Karabakh amid the Armenian population, Krunk became an influential force and, in the spring of 1988, expressed the true will of the

Karabakh Armenians. The society formed Committee 55, to which respected figures were elected. Soviet and Party powers were obliged to take account of their opinion. The Committee 55 chairman was Arkady Manucharov, the director of the Stepanakert building materials co-operative. (Later, in November 1988, he was arrested. In the indictment no political reason was cited. He was held on trumped up charges of corruption by a group of military personnel who arrived to arrest him in an armoured car in helmets and flak jackets.)

The decision of the Regional Committee of the Party, of which several members of Krunk were members, was considered a victory for the society. In Erevan the news was greeted with wild rejoicing. 6,000 Armenian refugees from Sumgait became witting or unwitting propagandists against Nagorny Karabakh remaining within Azerbaijan. The atrocities they spoke of gave rise to an anti-Azerbaijani mood. However, for the time being there were no acts of reciprocal violence from the Armenian side. Yet the situation was precariously balanced and any act could detonate an explosion.

Pravda published an article signed jointly by Ovcharenko, a Moscow journalist, and by their special Armenia correspondent, Arakelyan. As I have said, the article evoked a storm of protest in Armenia. *Pravda* was publicly burned in the street outside Arakelyan's flat and outside the newspaper's local office. Arakelyan took fright and sent a telegram to Afanasiev, the editor-in-chief of *Pravda*, dissociating himself from his published words and informing him that he had not authorised the piece for publication.

I asked Balayan whether Arakelyan was a party to the article or had *Pravda* just used his by-line?

'The article', said Balayan, 'included a quartet of my poems, constituting a sort of hymn to Karabakh. I know that Arakelyan insisted that they should name the author in the paper, so I'm sure Arakelyan was responsible and the paper did not forge his signature. I'm not even disputing facts now, but I'm grateful for the article. It poured salt on our wounds and kept us on our toes. All these events pushed us together and united us. It was very important, because the whole country was set against us, awaiting the events of the appointed day, 26 March. The foreign radio stations were all broadcasting about it. At home, my telephone was constantly engaged with calls from the West. I said I would not turn anyone away, although several times in the newspaper they warned me to behave more cautiously. But how could I refuse at a time of *glasnost* and *perestroika*? On 24 March in Moscow the Central Committee and the Council of Ministers gave out a decree concerning the socio-economic development of Karabakh. I knew that this was being prepared and warned our local Central Committee and Igor Muradyan that this announcement was intended to become law. And, indeed, up to now, they had been relying on it.

'While we were meeting, Azerbaijan did what it had to do. On the eve of 20 March I put a seven-page proposal to the Central Committee, proposing a road from Lachin to Stepanakert, an Armenian language television programme, schools, the restoration of Armenian historic monuments, etc.

'On 26 March the army was sent in to Erevan. Theatre Square was surrounded with tanks and over the town hovered helicopters nicknamed 'harbingers of *perestroika*'. Everyone was tense. But we decided,' continued Balayan, 'that no one should go out on the streets, not rise to the provocation. The soldiers were given cigarettes and flowers. And so on 26 March nothing happened. Everyone was amazed, indeed the whole world ... They rang me from Voice of America: "They say the town is as if dead." I replied, "I am standing at my window, I am putting the receiver out of the window and you can hear the noise of cars going by, hooters, people's voices." I put the telephone receiver outside and all of that went out on air. Then April went by in a wave of strikes.'

'How did the official circles in Armenia react?' I asked.

'You know, the people have never been so disenchanted by their leaders as they were then. And it was unpleasant to see these officials when, from time to time, they came to a meeting. They continued to believe that they had a passive audience, as they had had before. The bosses did not understand that after only a month the people could show political understanding, that their pride could be awakened. In those days I saw a lot of Demirchan, the first secretary of the Central Committee of the Communist Party of Armenia, and often said to him, "You have a big problem, which you don't recognise. You know superficially about psychology, but psychology means the science of the mind. But none of you understand that alongside cybernetics and genetics, social psychology was also stifled in its time. Without social psychology you cannot manage society and social change. Take one person – an individual really is a subject for psychology. Two people or more – that is already a qualitatively different human situation. When it comes to speaking to a crowd of 700,000, you have to feel humble before them, because they are the people and you are just one of them."'

'Didn't Demirchan understand that?'

'He should have understood, he had the facts. He knew that he had his whole office backing him up, behind him was the Russian secretary, the KGB. He was just talking like a landowner to his serfs. The people sensed it and shouted, "Strike!" but he said, "Do you think we're going to go on feeding you?" through clenched teeth and in Erevan slang too.

'It is obvious that social psychology can help a leader to read a situation. You arrive, let's suppose, at a wedding or a funeral and you must understand that the centre of attention at a wedding is the bride, at a funeral it is the corpse. Or for the sake of argument, say, Lenin went to one of Chaliapin's concerts. And suddenly the whole hall stood up and started applauding Lenin. Although he might have dreamed all his life of hearing Chaliapin, he would leave the hall so as not to upstage him, knowing he should not be the centre of attention on that particular occasion.

'A leader, knowing that he is always the centre of attention must conduct himself on every occasion in accordance with what is going on. The mood of the moment – that is what he must study. A time for throwing stones and a time for picking up stones – these are two entirely different moments. Funerals and weddings. You go to a stadium to watch football, you can shout at the top of your voice, take your tie off, like Ronald Reagan.

'When Reagan went to the funeral of the seven American astronauts, he was a completely different man. How he embraced the bereaved families! I don't think he was putting on an act. It was all very genuine. Our leaders haven't yet mastered those sort of occasions.

'The Karabakh movement highlighted the ineptitude of the republic's leaders. In the wolf pack the leader is chosen by natural selection. The lame and toothless are not suitable. It is unbearable to listen to our Secretaries talking about ideology,' continued Balayan. 'None of them realizes that they are boring. If only one of them would say: "Comrades, I have come to you with happy news. I have in my hands a proclamation about the unification of Karabakh and Armenia." Even then the people would not begin to listen. They want to hear those words from somebody they trust.'

Thus, instead of the expected mass meetings and speeches, the day of 26 March passed quietly. The army quit town, leaving the helicopters to carry out patrolling flights.

Behind the scenes, however, some who had grown used to activity did not want simply to await the Government's decision. The leaders of the Karabakh movement held meetings, but there were no speeches to the masses. Like every political movement in the process of development, the Karabakh movement began to review its slogans and its leaders. On a wave of popular confidence and freedom new names began to emerge, and speeches were made. These were totally unrealistic and mostly appealed to the far Left. Many sought popularity and a few attained it for a little while, diverting the people from decisions concerning the basic Karabakh issue.

Also on 26 March a certain man called Ayrikyan arrived in Erevan from Moscow. Although he had obtained an exit visa in January for himself, his wife and his three children, events in Armenia had kept him in the Soviet Union. From time to time he would give platform speeches demanding independence and the secession of Armenia from the Soviet Union. For all the revolutionary ardour of the people he addressed, they understood that Armenia is a frontier post of Christianity in the East; she has neighbours with whom she is linked by the same dreadful national memories and isolation is an unrealistic and possibly fatal concept for Armenians.

'What did you think, Zori – why did Ayrikyan come to Armenia on 26 March? I asked.

'Western journalists, mostly radio journalists who broadcast to Armenia, had made him a local star. He spoke very willingly and radically in public at the earliest opportunity. For that reason his speeches often concentrated on the atrocities, which would make him known as a saviour of the nation abroad.'

'If you knew that, so did the powers that be.'

'No, they didn't understand the situation. They arrested him and immediately Ayrikyan became a local hero. There and then a committee was formed to obtain his release. The world would forget about Karabakh and switch attention to Ayrikyan.'

'Is it possible that you are imagining all this?'

'From the start I have been suspicious of hangers-on. Every one of them saw himself in the movement rather than the movement itself. Nobody, apart from Igor Muradyan and his circle, wanted to sacrifice themselves. Ayrikyan was arrested. Even that worried me, because the crowd was already shouting for him rather than for Karabakh. Even if he had been Solomon himself I would have said that he was endangering the possibility of unification or, more correctly, the secession of Karabakh from Azerbaijan. You didn't have to be an oracle to see where all this Robespierrism would lead.'

Meanwhile, in Erevan, Armenian refugees continued to arrive from Azerbaijan. They were registered and some were sent to Karabakh, some stayed in Erevan and others were dispersed throughout the country.

Azerbaijan did not want the Armenian population of Karabakh to be increased, but many of the refugees were of Karabakh origin and it was difficult to refuse resettlement to Armenians frightened by the events in Sumgait.

In the Praesidium of the Supreme Soviet of the USSR, the chairmen of all the Supreme Soviets of all the republics condemned the Karabakh movement as 'destroying the friendship of our peoples'.

Pravda came out with an editorial against the case made by Nina Andreevna in *Soviet Russia*. Many politicians agreed that a clarification of the position would make Gorbachev's life easier, and they forecast the decline of Ligachev's star. Preparations were beginning for the nineteenth Party Conference, on which many new hopes were pinned. The theme of the conference also arose at renewed meetings in Erevan.

People were no longer meeting in the square but on the town hall steps. No less than 20,000 people gathered there.

Igor Muradyan remained, as before, head of the Karabakh Committee. However, there were more speakers addressing the audience in Armenian and he, not understanding the language, was no longer in control of the situation. Speakers talked of party corruption, accusing the Armenian party boss Demirchan (from whom Genrikh Pogosyan had by now taken over as head of the Communist Party of Armenia), about 'the mafia', about the Armenian atomic power station, about questions of ecology – they spoke about everything, but no meeting went by without a mention of Sumgait.

As before, people would gather if Muradyan named a day. Meetings on the steps became dangerous: too many people in too small a space. Muradyan called the next meeting and at the end he made a stupid mistake which would be used against him by his future enemies: 'Why are you criticising Demirchan here? If Demirchan hadn't been in charge, you don't know what would have happened on the twenty-sixth, what the tanks would have done. He did everything he could to avoid bloodshed and provocation, but all the same we keep hearing about Demirchan. Why should we be bothering about him? Even Kevorkov (secretary of the Karabakh Committee of the Party) isn't an issue as far as I am concerned. It still isn't clear how Kevorkov will be remembered.' He was whistled at for the first time.

24 April is the anniversary of the 1915 massacre of Armenians

by the Turks. Every year hundreds of thousands of people make a pilgrimage to the monument with flowers. A group from the Karabakh Committee hauled a stone cross there in memory of those who died in Sumgait.

Two days later, by government decree, the Karabakh Committee and the Krunk Society were disbanded. Without trying to be funny, Muradyan observed at a meeting: 'Our country is really extraordinary. They can even ban something which was never legitimized. Inasmuch as our committee has never been officially recognized, except by ourselves, we do not consider ourselves banned.'

Back in Karabakh at the May Day celebrations, where the usual platform had been erected on the town square stood the officials of the region: the first secretary of the Regional Committee, Pogosyan, and second secretary Malkov.

Suddenly the procession going past the platform came to a halt, a man stepped forward from the ranks and said that the procession would not move on until the officials had heard the crowd's slogans. People then stepped forward and spoke completely loyally (by the standards of the time and place) about *perestroika* and the unification of Karabakh.

Pogosyan raised his hand and said: 'I don't understand. Why are you hammering at an open door? Who told you that we weren't on your side? Who said that we had any aim other than the resolution of the Karabakh problem? We can only be with our Mother country. We must be freed from our present subordinate position.'

By the time he had finished speaking troops had surrounded the whole square shoulder to shoulder. One of the soldiers, finding himself on the platform, gave the order on his own authority that the troops should retire 200 metres.

In Erevan the month of May was spent in meetings. The basic question was the election of delegates to the Party conference. Speakers in front of large crowds did less to promote the cause of their preferred candidates and more to criticise the candidates put forward by the Party, accusing them together with the first secretary Demirchan, the President and the Prime Minister of the Republic of corruption and other crimes. Muradyan alone again defended Demirchan, although people were very critical of him and besides there were rumours that he was soon to be relieved of his post.

The subject of Sumgait did not die down. People were infuriated by the absence of any political reaction to the pogrom and by the first court hearings, at which the murderers were accused of aggravated hooliganism rather than contemplating genocide. The Baku papers available in Erevan published humiliating and, from the Armenian point of view, hostile articles about the unofficial leaders in Erevan. Moreover the Moscow media at that time were completely biased.

At the next meeting Muradyan said that people had to be ready to defend themselves because the Government did not guarantee their safety and stated that force had to be met with force. People were to arm themselves with sticks and Molotov cocktails; they had to defend themselves.

That evening at a closed session of the Karabakh Committee Muradyan was voted off. The committee wanted to act in constitutional fashion. Muradyan was deposed, but matters did not end there. Within two days, in the newspaper *Kommunist*, there was a leading article in which his call to arms was quoted. This obliged the Procurator's office to call Igor Muradyan to account.

'Muradyan came to ask what to do,' Balayan told me. 'We went to see the Procurator of the Republic, Suren Osipyan. Igor told him: "Kaputikyan and Balayan were with Gorbachev, who, in response to their appeal to settle the Karabakh problem, asked them if they had thought of the fate of the 270,000 Armenians living in Baku. The Government must consider their safety. We must consider whether our actions are justified and our requests lawful, not what the reaction might be to them. The Government has powers which can prevent law breaking. But Gorbachev's question had been put," continued Muradyan, "he could assess the situation clearly. That is why I said that we had to be ready to defend ourselves."

'Osipyan said to Muradyan, "You were inciting people to violence, which has not been done in Azerbaijan publicly. Your speech gives me grounds for prosecution."

'Igor wrote a letter of apology to the Procurator, as directed, and undertook that he would refrain from this theme in future.

'As we were coming out of the door', remembers Zori, 'I hit him hard. He is a big chap, too, 180 cm tall and weights 110 kilos, but I weigh in at 150 kilos. "Another two days and you'll ruin the whole movement," I remarked. They did not arrest him, but I knew that his fate had been decided by Osipyan, the Procurator. They came for him two months after that.'

At another meeting on 19 May people were waiting for Muradyan, but he was forcibly prevented from getting to the microphone. He tried to wriggle free, but at that moment a fellow from the Committee stepped out from the crowd. 'What has happened to the Armenian people? Can't you see that Igor Muradyan is a provocateur? For six weeks no one has spoken in the square. The militia were occupying it. Then, suddenly, they open the square. Don't you understand that the powers that be and the KGB are giving him the opportunity to lead you astray?'

This was not true, but Muradyan was prevented from defending himself. For a long time he disappeared from the political scene.

At the end of May changes took place in the administration of both republics. In the presence of Politburo members Yakovlev (in Erevan) and Ligachev (in Baku) Arutunyan and Vezirov were installed as first secretaries of the Central Committee of the Communist Party of Armenia. Their party careers had begun in the Komsomol, and both Vezirov early on and Arutunyan later had been secretaries of the Komsomol Central Committee and had worked in Moscow. Then Arutunyan had come back to hold a responsible position in Armenia, and Vezirov, having been for a short while the secretary of the Kirovabad town party committee, had been sent as Ambassador to Nepal and Pakistan. In official circles it was reckoned that they were clean (i.e. of bureaucratic corruption) because they had both lived for a long time outside their republics. Besides which, Arutunyan was one of those who had somehow made contact possible between the official powers and the movement. He would ask them what it was they wanted with the aim of arriving at a mutually acceptable solution. At that moment the Karabakh Committee and all the people greeted Arutunyan's appointment as a positive step. He seemed a completely democratic leader.

Balayan at this point distanced himself from the Karabakh Committee because, in his opinion, the problems of Karabakh were occupying less and less time on their agenda. Zori himself, as before, was devoted to the problems of Nagorny Karabakh, but he was regularly in Stepanakert.

I will leave Balayan for a while to occupy himself with his own affairs – we will meet him again in due course – but now our guide will be Doctor Galina Starovoitova, ethnographer and psychologist, whose subject is the history of the development of the Armenian movement. She knows its fundamental landmarks and leaders well.

By June, the emphasis of meetings began to change and attention was focused on the democratization of society, cleansing it of the influence of organized crime ('the mafia') and corruption. The people's deputies were required to be supporters of the Armenian desire for the unification of Armenia with Karabakh and, to this end, pressure groups were formed to convince them. Sometimes they were obliged to sign a declaration that they supported the idea of unification. Newspapers blamed activists in the movement for putting pressure on deputies and, although such pressure did not amount to blackmail, it was totally effective.

I know of an incident when one of the Party secretaries, another Muradyan, who was known to take bribes, refused to meet a deputation from a pressure group. Then activists blockaded his flat. He stopped coming home at night, so they simply followed him everywhere. Finally, they managed to stop his car on the street, they opened the door and shouted, 'Muradyan, get out.' He did so, but refused to sign the document confirming that he would vote for the motion for *Miatsum* in the Supreme Soviet.

Then someone in the crowd said: 'Didn't you know that he won't sign anything unless he gets a bribe? Come on, let's pay him.' And everyone started to shower him with rouble notes and coins. Then he signed.

For deputies who did not share local opinion about *Miatsum* signing such a document was not a simple matter, because many of them were bound by Party obligations not to support the decision of the Nagorny Karabakh Autonomous Region concerning unification with Armenia. A deputy often found himself between two stools. The official line was not to recognize the decision; the people's desire was to recognize it. Decisions were taken in the square and deputies were notified: either you express the will of the people or we will recall you. Meetings were accompanied by hunger strikes. Among the many on hunger strike, one man in particular stood out. He was a worker and a Hero of Socialist Labour called Manukyan. He got time off from work, told his wife that he was taking a holiday and went by himself to the square. Wearing a jacket with the star of a Hero and medals on his chest, he circulated among the other hunger strikers who were staying in the square so that they could not be accused of nipping away for a snack. A small, protected zone was reserved for them surrounded by flowers. From time to time, the excited Hero of Socialist Labour would jump up from his place and go to the microphone to say that in America Doctor Heider had said he was on hunger strike, but at night he ate and drank juice. Despite this, all the journalists clustered around Heider, while he, Manukyan, an honourable man, was on a real hunger strike – and not a single correspondent took the slightest interest in him.

On 15 June there was a session of the Supreme Soviet of the Armenian SSR. In Erevan troops were standing by. There was an enormous crowd in the square, some of whom were continuing the hunger strike, while others fainted from the heat. Soldiers' helmets were knocked off, there were heart-attacks, some people were carried out on stretchers.

The building of the Praesidium of the Supreme Soviet of Armenia was surrounded by several lines of troops. From the balconies of neighbouring houses people watched through binoculars to see what was happening inside the building. Undertakings had been obtained from almost all the deputies to vote for the motion, but nearly a million people were standing outside awaiting for the result. All roofs and even the trees were packed with waiting onlookers.

A member of the Karabakh Committee, a sixty-five-year-old candidate member of the Armenian Academy of Sciences, used his clout to get into the hall and said loudly: 'Now, chaps – you'll catch it if you don't vote in favour.'

'But that is putting on pressure,' I said to Starovoitova.

She laughed. 'But it was an honourable action. Our methods are totally constitutional.'

The session voted unanimously for unification, though it is possible that some did not attend the session.

Pandemonium broke out in the streets. Ambulances came to help those overwhelmed by the nervous strain. After the decision had been taken by the session, the hunger strike was called off. The hunger strikers were sent to hospital. The square was hosed down and cleaned up, as it was every time after such meetings.

Meanwhile, in Stepanakert, news of the Armenian Supreme Soviet decision was greeted with rapture. A moral victory had been won, a spiritual unification had been achieved. The most sober, however, understood that a real solution to the problem was still very far off, and there was one insuperable obstacle.

The session of the Supreme Soviet of Azerbaijan held on 17 June confirmed its previous position: it declared null and void the decision of the Karabakh people's deputies on 20 February. There was no need to prepare the public for this, since the interests of the deputies, of official politics and of the basic mass of Azerbaijanis were in no doubt whatsoever. Neither in Baku nor in Erevan did this decision evoke any particular reaction.

'In Azerbaijan there were still shock waves from Sumgait,' concluded Starovoitova. 'There was a desire to believe that people of "various nationalities" had died. Later two different lines of argument developed. One – a subtle one – was an explanation of Sumgait, but with remorse. The second was the result of a psychological mechanism whereby you project your own short-comings and faults on to others, thereby attributing your crime to the victims.'

But in Armenia they had decided they were right and the others were not.

A constitutional impasse arose. The sessions in Baku and Erevan appealed to different articles of the constitution. Article 70 states the basis for a multinational state, saying that it is a union of free, independent peoples or republics. Then there is Article 78, which is more precise and says that the borders of a republic cannot be changed without its consent. Azerbaijan relied on the more specific article and created a constitutional stalemate. For the first time they were trying to use the constitution, not as an ideological slogan, but as an instrument of genuine people-power, and it turned out that the articles of fundamental law were mutually contradictory both in spirit and in the letter. True, there had been previous similar situations, inasmuch as none of the articles are subordinated to the others. Meanwhile, towards the end of June, various informal movements came together as a united People's Front: they included the ecological 'green', religious and 'heritage' supporters as well as the Karabakh movement.

A meeting of the People's Front on 24 June was chaired by Silva Laputikyan. Balayan was present with several members of the Karabakh Committee and Starovoitova. The attempt to set up a People's Front was unsuccessful, since the specific Karabakh movement which had the unqualified support of the people did not permit the development of a People's Front along the Estonian model which Silva had studied. The Front did not emerge in a leading role and remained somewhat apart from the political mainstream.

Hardly were the events connected with the session of the Supreme Soviet over than work began on the preparation of nominations of delegates to the Nineteenth All Union Party Conference in Moscow. Galya Starovoitova said: 'I was on Theatre Square in Erevan at the end of June. Even when there wasn't a formal meeting, there were always plenty of people there, day or night, two or three hundred people would be standing around talking. Also Khadik Stamboltsyan would be there sitting behind his little table collecting signatures for nominations for delegates to the Party conference.'

Theatre Square was the centre of information and a form of symbolic ritual for gatherings there had developed. At the appointed hour columns would arrive from various regions under the tricolour flag. In contrast to the official flag on which three stripes alternated – red, blue and then red again – these flags had an orange stripe at the bottom: under a red sun and a blue sky, the orange earth. The flag was designed in 1881 by a member of the St Petersburg Armenian Society, Simon Gukasyan. Now it became a symbol of national unity. The columns arrived shouting '*Miatsum*' in unison. Three hundred or more people would stand in silence while a horn player played a beautiful two-minute melody taken from the theme song of an Armenian film, *The Sound of the River*. Over recent months people had begun to hum the tune while the horn played. For two minutes all these people would stand with clenched fists held aloft.

Another dramatic event occurred on 25 June. In the regional centre of Masis, twenty kilometres from Erevan, there was a mass poisoning of workers at a sewing factory, in a workshop where all the workers were Armenians except for two Azerbaijani women. These two women, having lodged a written complaint about their dismissal, left polyethylene packages and overalls at their work places. The overalls were moist and smelt of something. The fifty-one workers who remained in the shop began to feel suffocated, their heads ached, some of them who were pregnant later suffered miscarriages. It transpired that they had been poisoned by chloropeptin.

This event scandalised Armenia. Strikes began, coinciding with the Party conference, when all attention was focused on the Kremlin. The whole country held its breath, following the events unfolding there. The new thinking associated with the name of Gorbachev passed the test of firmness and durability in an eyeball-to-eyeball encounter with traditional Party ideology. Difficult topics cropped up there every day: now it was the press being anathematised, now a war of words; Yeltsin versus Ligachev, then the accusation by Ogonyok that four delegates had underworld criminal connections. With this great public event in the fore-ground the strikes and meetings in Erevan became of secondary interest, the more so because the mass media, as a rule, passed over them in silence.

In Armenia it was felt that their efforts to focus the attention of the general public on their struggle were dissipated in a con-spiracy of silence by television and newspapers. Resentment grew and so did the desire to shout out loud about what was going on. The strike became national. People now wanted decisions about everything: about Sumgait – to publish the names of all the victims, name the guilty men and bring the organizers, not just their henchmen, to justice; to declare what had happened in Sumgait to be genocide; to conduct a proper inquiry into what had happened in Masis; and finally to decide once and for all what was to happen about Karabakh ...

Events at the Party conference were followed on television in Erevan and the first secretary of the Communist Party of Armenia made a bad impression with his speech. In Theatre Square people began to talk of meeting their deputies returning from Moscow and having it out with them. Coincidentally, several of the unions working at Zvartnots airport decided to go on strike.

On the eve of the session of the Supreme Soviet of the USSR many feared that tensions would result in serious disorder with loss of blood. This would be dramatic for the Karabakh movement to the extent that it would change Soviet public opinion through-out the country, which was important for Armenia. Even if it did not worry anyone in the Baltic republics what effect the Estonians, Latvians or Lithuanians were producing on the rest of the USSR, because they were only appealing to their own people and to the West, in Armenia the reaction of the rest of the Soviet Union really mattered. The image of the movement had to be kept respectable. Certain journalists and historians with whom I spoke reckoned that Armenia hitting the headlines with an obvious breakdown of law and order would not have been totally unwel-come in the great game being played by the Soviet Government.

Disorders would even up the score between the Azerbaijanis and the Armenians, and would facilitate decision-making at the forthcoming session which, as will be seen, did little or nothing to untie this Caucasian knot.

Pavel Gutionov, an *Izvestiya* correspondent, met Galoyan, Vice-President of the Armenian Academy of Sciences, later secretary of the Armenian Communist Party, who told him that on 3 July he, Galoyan, had been to the Central Committee of Armenia with a group of academics to warn them that the intelligentsia feared possible provocations at Zvartnots airport. What Galoyan meant by 'provocations' was the stage management by Moscow of incidents which would give them an excuse to crack down on the Karabakh movement. In response the committee had reassured Galoyan that every precaution would be taken.

During a meeting in Erevan's Theatre Square on 4 July a man in the crowd shouted out, 'Lets go to the airport.'

Members of the Karabakh Committee in the square at the time went to the microphone and called for order: 'Stay where you are. This is a "provocation".'

The main body of people stayed put, but a group of several hundred continued to press the case for going off to the airport. Whereupon, somehow and prearranged by someone, a line of six buses appeared and the group got into them.

It would not have cost the powers-that-be or the troops who were all over town anything to detain these Icarus buses, but they were not stopped and soon arrived at the airport, where strike talks were going on. According to one account, some of the airport workers had decided to call off the strike; according to another, they had all agreed on a strike.

The new arrivals started to picket the ticket desks. Flights were delayed and soon the airport ground to a halt, though none of the demonstrators went out on to the tarmac. Soon the paras arrived and sealed off the building from the runway, leaving passengers in the waiting-room with the demonstrators.

That evening on national Soviet television the journalist Beketov's programme about Karabakh was shown. Various academics took part, among them the sociologist Jan Toschenko, who disgraced himself with his tendentious line. The whole of Armenia was incensed by their remarks. This one transmission played a major role in the kindling of passions.

That night the Deputy Minister for Internal Affairs, the secretary of the town Party Committee and members of the Karabakh Committee went to the airport for talks with the pickets. Top negotiators from both sides failed to come to an agreement, although the strikers did allow passengers out of the airport building and many Armenians offered to put up women and children in their own homes.

'I talked to the secretary of the Erevan town council, Mikhail Minasbekyan,' said Gutionov. 'He told me that the passengers had not been harmed in any way; at night cars brought food out for them. However, on the national evening news programme *Time (Vremya)* they complained that there was no milk for the children. As if Aeroflot conjures milk out of thin air for their youngest passengers every time a flight is delayed!'

At some time during 4 July the Ordzhonikidze Militia Academy was put on alert. Their commander, General Teodorov, was to complain later that Armenians had thrown stones at his officer cadets, who in the tragic days of Sumgait had come to the aid of Armenians. Meanwhile the troops on the ground sealed off the airport building. According to people who were there, crack squads of the MVD (Ministry of Internal Affairs), specially trained to deal with demonstrations, took part in this operation, although they received legal authority to do so only after the event, and there was never any official confirmation that they had taken part.

Next morning, the talks began again. The strikers understood the full seriousness of their action in seizing the airport and were prepared to organize a limited six-hour strike on condition that it would be called off if the *Time* evening news programme would carry an item on the seizure of the airport. Some of the demonstrators insisted on the continuation of the strike until the television broadcast began.

During talks with the troops a car suddenly appeared without warning on the runway just as a passenger plane was making its landing approach. Fortunately the plane avoided the car and, with great difficulty managed to land safely. This incident worried everyone who heard about it. True, lives had been endangered, but, despite some claims to the contrary, it had nothing to do with the strikers. According to hundreds of eye-witnesses who were asked about it later in court, the car belonged to the military.

Talks were continuing, when the MVD troops were ordered to clear the airport terminal. Armed with truncheons and shields, the soldiers rained blows on the unarmed crowd, regardless of whether they were strikers or waiting passengers.

'Did you see any of those who were beaten up?'

'I did,' replied Gutionov. 'In the hospital I met a chap who had eighteen lacerations. That means they didn't just hit him once, they gave him a real going over.'

Victims spoke of the savagery with which the troops 'evacuated' people from the airport. After the completion of their assault, the special squads boarded a plane and were flown off, leaving the officer cadets from Ordzhonikidze to patrol the airport.

'But the action was two-sided,' I said. 'It's known that the strikers threw stones at the soldiers.'

'When the MVD troops entered the building,' replied Gutionov, 'the pickets did not have stones with them. They mockingly clapped the soldiers, even kneeling in front of them. The stone-throwing started after the officer cadets had cordoned off the building. Insided this cordon the officer cadets started to hustle groups towards the main Echmiadzin road. A military guard truck from the atomic power station was driving along it at the time, fully loaded. The crowd stopped it, attacked the driver and the corporal co-driver. The soldier driver ran away and hid in an Armenian house, but the corporal reached for a gun and shot Khachik Zakharyan, a student, in the head. Within an hour, he was dead. For a long time it was impossible for an ambulance to get through the cordon of troops. Eventually, the wounded were loaded on to first-aid cars. But they didn't take them to hospital; they took them to the square, where a meeting was in progress. There the battered strikers from the airport interrupted the meeting with shouts of, "They're beating up our people."

'The sight of their wounded comrades electrified the crowd,

which quickly decided to deal the troops a blow. What would have happened if the 300,000 strong crowd had indeed reached the airport where armed soldiers were deployed on active service beggars the imagination.

'Ashot Manucharyan came to the microphone. "Don't allow this to kindle a hatred of Russians. This wasn't done by the Russians. This was done by the powers that be. Power doesn't have nationality. So, I now want you to disperse in an orderly way." And the crowd dispersed.

'Cars, decorated in black funeral flags, began to race through the town at top speed with their horns blaring. The noise reached such a pitch that the soldiers had to put cottonwool in their ears. Students piled the classics of Marxism-Leninism in a circle and walked round inside them as if in a prison yard, their hands behind their backs. The soldiers kept their distance. The aeroplane from Moscow carrying the Party Conference delegation, due to land at Erevan, landed at Kirovakan instead.

'The casualties on both sides were counted up the following day: 3 officer-cadets had various injuries, and 36 civilians, 12 of them women, were hospitalized.

'The population of the USSR heard about these events from the television reports by B. Baryshnikov. From these they gathered that the troops had behaved themselves bravely and politely, and that their opponents were a band of hooligans. Viewers were shown two wounded soldiers, but not a single civilian. The *Time* programme showed an item from Zvartnots featuring a passenger from Tallinn. The interviewer asked him: "You were a witness to these events. What can you tell us about the actions of the strikers occupying the airport?" He replied that he had "never dreamed of witnessing such scenes in the Soviet Union." The reporter commented on this phrase as a man-in-the-street's condemnation of the actions of the demonstrators.

'At the television station in Erevan, where they edited the item, they were able to transcribe from the tape the full text of the man from Tallinn's reply and on the following day, during the interval between the first and second parts of the film of *Hamlet* on Armenia's television channel, they showed the complete interview. This revealed that the second half of the sentence after the phrase about him never imagining that such things were possible in the Soviet Union continued: "that Soviet soldiers could beat up completely defenceless people like that".

'After this revelation the MVD, worried by the incensed reaction of the population, began to prepare a programme in which they intended to prove how aggressive the crowd had been.

'We were also shown on television a mountain of knives, sticks and other weapons,' continued Pavel Gutionov. 'The fact is that not one of these weapons was found at Zvartnots. They were confiscated from the drivers of cars on the highways patrolled by the military leading out of town.'

The events at the airport were corroborated by many of the people with whom I spoke. From what they added, I shall single out the information given to me by the special correspondent of *Moscow News*, Andrei Pralnikov. He heard that on 6 July there had been a brawl between the paras guarding the airport runways and groups of the MVD. The quarrel was ideological. It began with the paras blaming the militia for unjustified brutality against the unarmed populace. The conflict was settled by a third force, which disarmed both the paras and the MVD. There was no official information available on this subject. However, even if this story was invented, it shows a characteristic desire of the Armenians to divide the soldiers into good and bad ones. Up to that time, they were all more or less good – they would give them food, cigarettes and so on.

Control over the national press was maintained on the spot by a party bureaucrat named Sevruk, who, in order to emphasise the severity of the situation, went about the town in an ex-Afghan combat suit, summoning journalists to briefings every day to give them the following confidential instruction: their reporting was to be wholly governed by the decisions of the Nineteenth Party Conference on the nationalities question.

On 11 July the funeral of Khachik Zakharyan took place. His

coffin was borne round the streets and squares, followed by a mass of people.

At the head of the funeral procession walked the founder of the charity Mercy, forty-eight-year-old Khachik Stamboltsyan, a worker at the Institute of Experimental Biology. Through a megaphone he pacified the crowd with a Christian message: 'We were the first Christian state on earth. I do not ask you to have peace in your hearts, although maybe peace is what we most need. I ask you to keep faith that we will find peace in another world. We will not despair and we will not let bitterness enter our hearts.'

People gave way, parting to let the coffin through. The soldiers watched quietly, not interfering with the procession.

The 15th of July was the appointed day of the meeting of the Praesidium of the Supreme Soviet of the USSR, after which it would become clear which of the decisions of the Supreme Soviets – of Azerbaijan or of Armenia – would be supported by the central Government.

The decision was never really in doubt. What interested people was how the decision would be announced and how the Armenian leaders would acquit themselves in the presence of the most important VIPs in the country. A rumour crept through Erevan that the meeting had really begun on the 14th and continued until the following day; and there were fresh rumours about the heroism of the delegation and of hopes of the resolution of the question in favour of Armenia and Karabakh.

On the day of the meeting the streets were empty – everyone was at home by their television sets. The speech by the first secretary of the Nagorny Karabakh Regional Committee of the Party, Genrikh Pogosyan, confirmed the unity of the administrators of Karabakh with their people. The Armenian party workers, cultural leaders and scientists insisted upon unification. However, Mikhail Gorbachev's remarks and the speeches of the Azerbaijani representative and those from other republics all made it clear that Armenia was not going to win this round.

Television sets were hurled through windows into the streets. There were no casualties.

Galina Starovoitova was in Erevan at the time. 'In general things were calm. Of course, lots of letters were published and read out on the air. Their tone was more or less the same.'

'Did they criticise the Praesidium?'

'There were two themes. One is shown fairly clearly in a letter from a very old writer, Sero Khanzadyan. I quote from memory: "My fellow countrymen, we have seen how our little hero Genrikh Pogosyan, steady as a rock of Karabakh, and how our eagle Sergo Ambartsumyan ... (a list of others followed), how all of these have been thrown under the wheel of the ruthless carriage of state", etc. This theme of heroic behaviour is characteristic of the reaction as far as Gorbachev was concerned. Another theme was "These Brezhnevite bootlickers Gromyko [President of the USSR] and Shcherbitsky [first secretary of the Communist Party of the Ukraine] – how dare they pass judgement on the suffering and needs of our people".'

'Were there criticisms of Gorbachev's behaviour at the meeting of the Praesidium of the Supreme Soviet?'

'Not that I heard. He remained a figure of authority who was being misled by the "bootlickers" and the "mafiosi".'

On 18 July more troop reinforcements were transported to Erevan. Disorder was expected as a result of the publication of the decisions of the Praesidium of the Supreme Soviet of the USSR, which ruled out the unification of Karabakh with Armenia. In Moscow, Alexander Yakovlev, a key figure in the reform movement, explained to journalists that any boundary changes would bring about an explosive situation at no fewer than eighteen other points of intercommunal tension within the USSR. It was becoming clear that the nationalities question no longer fitted the slogans 'Friendship between peoples' and 'Internationalism'. Nationalist politics were entering a most acute phase.

In Erevan, meanwhile, there was a meeting on 20 July in the Matenadaran (which houses the Armenian national library), at which the decision of the Praesidium was unanimously rejected.

At this time the wave of strikes was dying down. There were no public meetings. Armenia seemed to be mulling over what had happened and developing fresh ideas. '*Miatsum*' was yesterday's slogan. Now there was a new word: '*Anzhatum*' – secession from Azerbaijan.

This is an appropriate moment to discuss the six alternative possibilities for settling the Karabakh problem. Galya Starovoitova sees them thus:

1st option: To grant the status of autonomous republic to Nagorny Karabakh, but leave it within the boundaries of Azerbaijan. This would allow Karabakh to adopt its own constitution and settle the question of its official language. There could be two, Armenian and Azerbaijani. For example, in Abhazia, which is within the boundaries of Georgia, there are three official languages altogether: Abkhazian, Georgian and Russian. This option would have been a good one up until the tragic events in Sumgait or immediately after it. Now it is too late.

2nd option: Condominium status, like Anglo-Eygyptian Sudan, with stripes on the map and dual administration/government – in our case Azerbaijani and Armenian. Insofar as the population within each district of Karabakh is overwhelmingly of one nationality, it would be possible to choose people's committees for each region with an orientation towards each of their respective parent republics. Four of the districts would have been oriented towards Armenia, and the fifth towards Azerbaijan. Within each district there could have been more of a mix. This possibility is all the more relevant since there is now talk once again of people's rural committees, which did exist up to 1932, but were destroyed by Stalin. Within the ambit of these relatively small groups of people decisions could be taken about language policy, schools and so on.

3rd option: Presidential rule. For example, in the state of Punjab in India or the southern states of the USA during the period of reconstruction after the Civil War. It was precisely because of racial conflict that they were placed directly under the President. What would happen is Nagorny Karabakh would be taken from Azerbaijan but not given to Armenia. A special precedent would be created, of an autonomous republic which was governed directly by the Supreme Soviet of the USSR for, let us say, one or two five-year periods. Meanwhile, the economy and culture would have a chance to revive. Then carry out a referendum.

(This conversation with Galya Starovoitova took place after the creation of a special governing committee for Karabakh. For this reason, some of the questions I put to her break the continuity of the chronology of events, but preserve the logic of the conversation.)

'Galya, was what happened in January close to this version?'

'Not entirely. The committee of special government has been created. It is answerable to Moscow. But under which criminal code will criminals be arraigned? Evidently, according to Azerbaijani law. In the autumn of 1989 will there be elections to the Supreme Soviet of the republic. To whom will the Karabakh deputies answer? The actions of all our democratic institutions are suspended. There is a regional committee of the Party, but there is no first secretary [Pogosyan was sacked]. The whole set-up depends on a heavy military presence. So it is not clear what sort of socio-economic structure there really is.'

'It is clear that the present set-up can only be provisional. What other alternatives are there?'

4th option: Bearing in mind that the right to self-determination is a higher form of state sovereignty, this would mean making some necessary changes to the Constitution in order to meet the demands of both Nagorny Karabakh and Armenia. This option has still not been ruled out, but its realization has been seriously affected by the fact that within Azerbaijan a separate political process has been going on. They have developed their own solutions to the problem as well as their own demands: to disband the Nagorny Karabakh region as a whole, to arrest Balayan, Pogosyan and all the ringleaders; to create a form of national autonomy for the 200,000 Azerbaijanis living in Armenia; to send those accused of the atrocities in Sumgait for trial in Baku rather than in Moscow or Voronezh. Ecological demands were also expressed, as well as a campaign for the use of Arabic script [in Azerbaijan the cyrillic alphabet is used at present].

A tremendous ethnic solidarity has fast developed among all Azerbaijanis. It somehow gained impetus from the worsening of the situation, because their consciousness was raised in step with the quickening tempo of events. There were the first signs of unofficial movements, even if they were a pretty mixed bunch.

5th option: A territorial swap. To give back Karabakh to Armenia and to Azerbaijan those parts of Armenia with significant Azerbaijani populations, such as the Megriisky region. True, this is a very important Christian wedge between the two halves of Azerbaijan as well as the border between Iran and Turkey. This option is not really a starter because it entails the manipulation of people without obtaining their consent.

6th option: An armchair solution: to change the boundaries on the basis of a plebiscite. Long strips on either side of the border are envisaged as the demarcation (target) zone. Within these strips of land, carry out a referendum, on the basis of which the land would be allocated to one or the other republic.

Back in Armenia a stormy July was drawing to a close. After the strikes people were going back to work. On the eve of a quiet August there was an important event: the Praesidium of the Supreme Soviet of the USSR issued two ukases, one concerning the regulations governing the organization of meetings and demonstrations, and the second concerning the rights and duties of troops with so-called 'special duties'.

Until then, meetings, demonstrations and processions had not been against the law. Now, to hold any gathering, a permit had to be obtained from the mayor's office in Erevan. They usually gave the Karabakh Committee permission to hold meetings.

(Meetings indeed started again on 31 August and hardly stopped until the earthquake in December). But sometimes the Committee held unsanctioned meetings for which they were summoned to appear in court. They did not answer the summons. The first time, they were given a fine, which they did not pay, and warned that a second offence could mean up to six months' imprisonment.

From the beginning of September the activity of the whole Karabakh movement sharply increased.

In Karabakh itself all this time a strike had been in progress. All work had stopped except farming. The harvest was unusually good. In previous years, Karabakh had given more than eighty per cent of its agricultural produce to Azerbaijan. This year it gave nothing. Officials from the Azerbaijan republic departments were not allowed anywhere near. The barns were filled. The region would be able to hold out all winter.

At about this time a group of industrial managers and directors of various local concerns which had been formed to replace the disbanded Krunk society – a group to which for all practical purposes all the local leaders belonged – decided to call a general strike. The strike was accompanied by meetings demanding secession from Azerbaijan. Popular participation was as high as ever, but they were growing sick and tired of the Karabakh movement and of the People's Front, which was preoccupied with illogical problems, the battle against the 'mafia', and the question of democratization, whilst the Karabakh question was forgotten. Ties were being broken. Only Zori Balayan never forgot for one second about Karabakh. He commuted between Stepanakert and Erevan with the message: 'Do not forget about Karabakh.'

In the middle of September, Karabakh woke up again.

On 18 September there was an open clash between the Armenian and the Azerbaijani populations of the Nagorny Karabakh region.

On that day in Stepanakert, there was an officially sanctioned town meeting, dedicated to the memory of the twenty-six Bolshevik commissars of Baku who were arrested in July 1915 and shot by counter-revolutionaries, and to the memory of the Armenian victims of the 1915 Turkish massacre in Baku.

In the Azerbaijan village of Khodzhalu local people stopped three Armenian cars loaded with beds and bedding for the soldiers in Stepanakert, and stoned the cars and drivers, among them a Russian lieutenant who was with the convoy. After that they left them in the road. Several Zhiguli cars (the main road goes straight through the centre of the village) tried to pick them up, but these cars were also attacked. Two of the Armenian cars got away and drove to Stepanakert. The beaten-up drivers explained what was happening and several hundred men in buses and lorries, armed with axes and hunting rifles, set off for Khodzhalu. Near the village they were stopped by soldiers, who prevented some of the group from going any further. Some, however, broke through to Khodzhalu, where they were met with rifle fire. A following car had meanwhile been ambushed in the village. The passengers were fired on and beaten with iron bars. In all, as a result of the fracas, 25 people were taken to hospital, 19 with bullet wounds, 7 with knife wounds and the rest with a variety of other injuries.

There was shooting not only in Khodzhalu but also in a village on the outskirts of Stepanakert called Kirkidzhan. In this village two Armenian houses and one Azarbaijani house were set on fire; fortunately no one was hurt.

In Stepanakert several Azerbaijani houses were attacked, stones were thrown through windows. A young musician was severely wounded by a knife wound in the back, and three Azerbaijanis were arrested. They were taken to hospital and thence more or less immediately removed for safety to Shusha. That night, at the request of the region's leaders, including the all-powerful A. I. Volsky of the USSR Supreme Soviet and the Central Committee, a group of specialist doctors was flown by charter flight from Erevan to Stepanakert to provide medical help on the spot.

The situation was near breaking point. In Stepanakert wounded people were brought in from various settlements, amongst them fourteen Azerbaijanis. Volsky declared a curfew with all the inevitable consequences in Stepanakert, Shusha and Khodzhalu. Meetings were forbidden. It was not permitted to be on the street between 9 p.m. and 7 a.m. Local people began to organize vigilante groups which patrolled the houses round the clock.

★   ★   ★

On 19 September the first secretary of the Communist Party of Azerbaijan, A. Vezirov, gave his version of events to Baku party activists, summarized thus. There was a meeting in Stepanakert, where extremist voices were raised. 'We're fed up.' 'We've had enough.' Fights even broke out amongst the people attending the meeting. In the middle of all this came the electrifying news from arriving Zhiguli car drivers that Armenians were being beaten up in Khodzhalu. As it happened, several trucks with the word 'Armenia' written along their sides had been stopped for inspection and a scuffle broke out between some corporals of the MVD and members of the so-called 'construction gangs' on board from Erevan. This was witnessed by several passing Zhiguli drivers. Troops succeeded in stopping some of the group which had boarded buses and trucks, but some managed to break through the military roadblock and got to the village. They set fire to haystacks and houses. Shots from hunting rifles were fired. The troops regained control, and the pogrom turned back and attacked the little hamlet of Kirkidzhan on the outskirts of Stepanakert itself.

The casualties, according to Vezirov, included 24 men, 20 of them Armenians, one of whom, a seventy-year-old carpenter, subsequently died in hospital. There was a very tense atmosphere in Shusha, where many Azerbaijanis fled to escape the pogrom. Rumours about an Armenian church being burned down were, according to Vezirov, a malicious lie.

Steps were being taken to pacify the population. They had had difficulty in keeping the crowd in Agdam from setting out for Khodzhalu. A meeting to discuss how to protect Azerbaijanis took place in the central square of Nakhichevan. In Baku, Sumgait, Kirovabad and other places in Azerbaijan there were no incidents whatever, apart from two explosions at factories in Sumgait heard several days before. Further inquiries revealed that in one of the consignments of raw material despatched to the factory from Krasnodar there were ten kilos of explosive ammoniac potassium nitrate.

During his speech to the activists in Baku, Vezirov warned everyone present to be exceptionally careful and alert.

News of what had happened reached Erevan late on the evening of 19 September. All night the streets of the city were thronged. Demonstrators demanded that immediate measures be taken to 'save their fellow countrymen in Karabakh'. In the morning, Voskanyan, the President of the Armenian Republic, made a speech and tried to calm people down, but the demonstrators demanded the convocation of an extraordinary session of the Armenian Supreme Soviet.

In the evening, there was a meeting attended by virtually every adult in the town. A national strike was declared. Students continued with their hunger strike.

Thereafter meetings continued every day. It was at about this time that the Karabakh movement turned on the local 'mafia'. Going further than the question of whether to press for unification or secession, the Karabakh movement had in the summer already been calling for democratization and social reform. Since some seats were vacant in the Armenian Supreme Soviet, the Karabakh Committee decided to put up candidates.

At a meeting on 1 October the Committee suggested that people should cross out the following from the official list of candidates on their voting slips: Mkrtychyan, the minister of Foreign Affairs, and Arutunyan, minister of Internal Affairs, and substitute instead Khachik Stamboltsyan, chairman of the Armenian charity Mercy (born in 1940, a scientist in the Institute of Experimental Biology), and Ashot Manucharyan, a member of the Karabakh Committee (born in 1954, graduated in physics from Erevan University, then secretary of the Komosomol committee at the university and deputy director of school No. 122).

Elections took place the following day. About eighty per cent of the voters wrote on their voting slips the names of the movement's candidates, but the Government did not recognize the elections as valid because the winners were not included on the official list of candidates.

At the next meeting the voters asked for the result of the ballot. Meetings continued until 8 October, when the election committee recognized Stamboltsyan's election.

However, on 10 October, the office of the Central Committee

of the Armenian Communist Party reversed the decision of the election committee, accusing its chairman, Kh. Mandalyan, of falsifying the results. Mandalyan, a secretary of the Erevan city soviet, was expelled from the Party and his expulsion was announced on the national television evening news programme *Vremya*.

This led to a new outbreak of unrest; meetings and demonstrations started.

A re-run of the election was announced. Put up as opponents of the rebel candidates were two outstanding people: People's Artist of the Soviet Union Sos Sarkisyan, a man with a clear conscience and unusually popular, and Shavarsh Karapetyan, a past world champion in underwater swimming, a man of great courage and self-sacrifice, who had beome a hero after a tragic accident, when a trolleybus full of passengers fell over a dam into a reservoir. Finding himself on the scene by chance, Shavarsh alone saved more than twenty people. He was also a friend of Balayan.

These two men were truly worthy of sitting in the Armenian parliament. Not wishing, however, to create an opposition to the Karabakh movement, Sos Sarkisyan and Shavarsh Karapetyan withdrew their candidature on the day before the elections, when it was too late to nominate new candidates. Khachik Stamboltsyan and Ashot Manucharyan were therefore elected deputies of the Supreme Soviet of Armenia.

The Party apparatus and bureaucracy became nervous at the election of two leaders of the Karabakh movement. To discredit the unofficial leaders, the idea of linking them with the local 'mafia' was born. Thus a particular Armenian social scientist prepared for general consumption ideologically compromising material on the Karabakh movement. From the summer of 1988 onwards, this idea surfaced from time to time in the newspapers and on television, but not one member of the 'mafia' was ever actually discovered in the movement despite the most thorough detective work.

Apart from that, Ashot Manucharyan was offered 200,000 roubles by total strangers to resign. When Manchuryan refused, they raised their offer, explaining that the original bribe was just an opening bid. When he refused a second time, they threatened to beat him up.

The Karabakh movement doubtless possesses significant information concerning the influence of powerful criminals in the republic's administration at all levels, about enormous bribes, about organized crime in which members of the Party administration-boss clan are involved. It is possible that more will come out following private inquiries by the movement.

At the beginning of October a commission of the Soviet of Nationalities of the Supreme Soviet of the USSR arrived in Stepanakert. According to evidence given to me, the visitors from Moscow came to the conclusion that secession from Azerbaijan was essential, although the form it might take and the extent of its dependence on the republic remained unclear.

In the people's court of Sumgait the visiting Voronezh assizes began its work on 12 October. The case was heard against Mekhdiev, Rzaev and Turabiev – three of the ninety accused of rioting, murder, rape, arson and looting.

Representatives of the victims arrived in Sumgait with their lawyer, Reuben Saakyan, though the proceedings did not get under way immediately. To begin with, one of the victims was missing and also the defendants rejected two lawyers. Then the defence counsel asked for time to study the case in detail.

On 14 October, before the hearing began, local residents threatened the victims with reprisals. A member of the observer group from the Soviet state prosecution service, Valeev, took the Armenians to a safe place, where the observer group from Moscow was staying. That same day, the entrance door to the block of flats where one of the victims lived in Baku was marked with a cross.

The court building was heavily guarded; ranks of militia reinforced the usual police escorts. Proceedings got under way on 24 October, but within a day, the victims' side, not satisfied by the proposed charges, left the courtroom, refusing to take part in the trial or give evidence and asking that Saakyan be excused from taking part in the proceedings.

'On the eve of the preparatory hearings, before the charges had been read out, I had asked the court to order further inquiries,' said Saakyan. 'Mekhdiev had not been charged with incitement, murder and rape. Rzaev was charged with the murder of Avanesyan and incitement to murder his brother, but it had not been mentioned that the murders had been carried out with particular brutality. The victims were not presented with all the suspects for identification. There were seventeen objections in all.'

'Is it true that the victims asked for the hearings to be transfered to Voronezh?'

'Yes. They and several witnesses were afraid to give evidence in Sumgait, the very place where completely innocent people had been killed right in front of their eyes, women raped, flats ransacked, men and women stripped naked, paraded through the streets, humiliated and mocked, and stones thrown at troops, cars overturned and set alight.'

The state lawyers and the prosecutor rejected Saakyan's submission. One can imagine how the victims felt about this decision. They suspected that the court would conceal the true facts which they had witnessed with their own eyes and that the guilty men, even those found guilty by the court, would not be sentenced for their crimes according to the law. What can they have thought when Mekhdiev's defence counsel said that his case should be 'transfered to be tried before a people's court'?

'In this court, as in the Soviet High Court, the offences committed at Sumgait were described as "hooliganism". Was that a fair description?' I asked Saakyan.

'The investigating authorities acted according to the court criminal code. This repeated use of the term "hooliganism" derived from the only possible legal approach to the Sumgait tragedy. It had to be treated as one criminal event consisting of many parts. The absence of a more appropriate formula in the criminal law obliges lawyers to consider the affair as one complex crime consisting of the sum of murders, rapes, arson attacks, robberies and looting, rather than as separate crimes which just happen to have all taken place at the same time.'

'Has your view been confirmed by witnesses' evidence?'

'There is much evidence which has yet to be thoroughly examined by the court.'

The accused, witnesses and people in authority, basically all Azerbaijanis, had given evidence during the investigation that Mekhdiev, one of the organizers of the pogrom, in his incitements to violence against the Armenians had said: 'Are you not Muslims? In Armenia they are raping Azerbaijani women, cutting off their breasts, stripping them naked, leading them through the streets, branding them with crosses on their foreheads and that is why we must kill Armenians, wipe them off the face of the earth . . .'

'Surely you have to have nerves of steel to be able to listen to that nightmarish stuff day after day?'

'A man could go mad reading the evidence. In the course of an hour, after breaking down the door of the Avanesyans' flat, throwing stones through the window and trying to set fire to the flat, they hit the stepfather on the head with a rock. He fell, unconscious. His wife dragged him up to the first floor, to a flat occupied by a Russian family. The brothers, Albert and Valery, tried to escape, but each of them separately was surrounded by a mob armed with spears, stones, knives and clubs with which they were brutally put to death.'

Reading the evidence in the case, I was astonished by the submissions of the Azerbaijani lawyer concerning the episode of the murder of Albert Avanesyan by Turabiev. According to Turabiev's defense lawyer, Turabiev found himself at the scene of the incident by chance and, seeing that many people were holding Albert by his arms and, assuming he was an Armenian, he struck him with his penknife with the aim of frightening him; Albert didn't even flinch from the blow and remained standing. The lawyer concluded his remarks as follows: 'Turabiev did not intend to kill Avanesyan. Based on the foregoing, there is no evidence in the actions of Turabiev of intent to commit a premeditated crime as defined in Articles 72 and 94 p.2 of the criminal code of the Azerbaijan Soviet Socialist Republic. I therefore ask that the criminal charge be dismissed.'

A witness for the prosecution in Turabiev's case known as M. K. not only gave evidence about how he had kicked her but also how she and her sister were raped in their flat by dozens of Azerbaijanis. Then, said M. K., she was led naked through the streets of the town and was subjected to further beatings and humiliation. The case in connection with this rape was at the enquiry stage. Many of those guilty of the rape, according to M. K., were arrested.

'How do you assess the actions of the local representatives of the Ministry of Internal Affairs [i.e. the MVD]?' I asked Saakyan.

'I consider that the behaviour of the Sumgait militia was nothing less than criminally negligent. That is the only way to describe it'.

Saakyan's opinion is supported by the evidence of an Azerbaijani witness: 'Near me were four militia men – all sergeants – and two firemen. They were making no attempt whatever to intervene. Two Armenian brothers ran out of the entranceway surrounded by a mob. Valery ran towards the pumping station, but Albert ran towards the recruiting office (the distance between the two would be about fifty metres). About ten men surrounded Valery and began beating him up. He fell and they continued their attack on him. This went on for about five minutes, until he stopped moving and showed no sign of life. Not one of the militia men attempted to help him. Even the fire engine, which was pulling out of the fire station, nearly ran him over. One of the militia said that it was useless to try and help him, since he was going to die anyway. I was extremely suprised that such a thing could take place in front of four armed militia men in uniform, and that they did not attempt to help a man who was being beaten to death. I walked on, and from a distance of five metres I could see that he was still moving and breathing heavily. I went up to one of the militia men and told them that he was still alive. One of them replied that he would die in any case and told me to leave the courtyard. I saw that ten men were beating Albert outside the recruiting office. He was screaming. I did not go near, but I could see that they were going to kill him too. Militia men were also watching that.'

A victim, Khachatur Babaev, at risk to his own life, slid down the drainpipe from the third floor of his home and ran to the second division of the militia opposite his house and told them what was happening. Ten or twelve militiamen were sent to the house. They did not go in, but went off somewhere else. At this very moment, the mob was trying to throw Babaev's wife out of the third-floor window, having stripped her naked. One of them was trying to cut off the lobe of her ear to get her earring. It has been established that at the time there was a group of militia in the yard of Babaev's house, led by a man of senior rank, an MVD colonel who 'by dint of tremendous effort' succeeded in persuading Mekhdiev to exert his influence on the mob and call off the attack on the Babaev's flat.

The final assessments were held in Moscow at the Supreme Court of the USSR and likewise took place without the participation of the Armenian victims or their lawyers, although they had lodged a series of demands. Their three main demands were: to call as witnesses Muslim-Zade, the Secretary of Sumgait town soviet, and General Kraev, who had been in charge of suppressing the riot, so that they could confirm the organized nature of the actions of the mob; to set aside the sentences from separate courts and re-hear the case in one unified trial; and to charge those who took part in the pogrom under Article 67 of the criminal code of Azerbaijan (which corresponds with Article 74 of the Russian Soviet Federated Socialist Republic code), i.e. incitement to racial hatred.

Although the events in Sumgait come under the category of genocide according to the international convention of 1948 signed by the USSR, under Soviet law there is no such crime; nor is there a word for it in the criminal code. Genocide cannot be alleged as state policy but only as the actions of individuals. (*Izvestiya* published an article about bandits killing some Indians in Brazil and called that 'genocide'.)

After consideration, the court refused all these requests except the last, conceding that in the course of preparatory investigations (although they lasted longer than the preparations for the Nuremberg trials) not all the details of the case had been studied.

The cases of three further accused, Izmailov, Djafarov and Akhmedov, were separated. One remained in court, while the others were led away to help with inquiries into other incidents, because this case concerned events in District 41a. The court considered that it was not necessary to call General Kraev and Muslim-Zade, since there was sufficient evidence already on the case.

At this time, the sworn testimony of the secretary of the Nagorny Karabakh district committee of the Party, Genrikh Pogosyan, arrived in Moscow from Stepanakert. In other circumstances, this could have brought about a U-turn in the court, because of its sensational nature, but it was not brought in evidence in the case. Pogosyan testified that during the plenum of the Central Committee of the Communist Party of Azerbaijan in May, Muslim-Zade, who was being expelled from the Party, claimed in self-justification that in Sumgait he, as the secretary of the town council, was only carrying out the orders of the administration and was not himself guilty of anything. (He is now the director of a co-operative in Baku.)

Furthermore, the court refused to charge any of the accused with incitement to racial hatred (although in evidence it was shown that Akhmedov had walked around with a megaphone shouting, 'Muslims, kill Armenians!') on the basis that it would supplant a more severe criminal charge, i.e. of murder. This sounded absurd, because an indictment should include everything of which a defendant is accused. Besides, it avoided any moral or political evaluation of the Sumgait events.

The victims submitted written statements to the effect that they considered the trial to be biased and incompetent, and that they therefore refused to take part in it, dismissing their lawyers with thanks for their conscientious work. Then all the Armenians present stood up and left the court. Judge Brize immediately announced an adjournment until the following day.

At the entrance to the High Court on Vorovsky Street stood a small crowd of Armenians who had not been allowed into the courtroom. Amongst them was Nagapetyan, who had aspired to the role of national leader in Moscow. (In May he had promoted the idea of Armenia as a non-Party republic and even recruited followers who all deposited their Party cards in the same safe.

They had decided to wait and see how things turned out, then they would decide whether to stay in or resign.) The group standing on the street suddenly produced tricolour flags and banners which read 'Shame on the High Court' and, shouting, 'Rubbish, rubbish', they quickly dispersed. The militia guarding the building hardly had time to react.

A friend of Zori Balayan and my friend Armen Oganesyan showed me a statement which had been written at the time of the trial in Moscow by Karina, the bereaved fiancée of one of the Melkumyan family, five of whom had been killed at Sumgait:

> Dear Judges,
>
> We have lost our nearest and dearest. Some of us have literally lost everyone. The prisoners in the dock are three criminals who are trying to escape their just deserts by any means they can, brazen and defiant. For us and for you too the terrible fact must be obvious that they are not ready even inwardly to admit their dreadful crimes. During the course of the trial it has become quite obvious that these three alone – one of whom is not yet an adult – could not have rioted, killed and raped whole areas of the town, setting fire to houses, the living and the dead. Does it not occur to you to ask where are the hundreds of others who were the real organizers of this terrible crime not only against Armenians but against the whole of the Soviet Union, and the whole of mankind?
>
> In the Soviet press there has been a report of a trial in Brasilia concerning five criminals who killed three Indians. Our press describes this as 'genocide'. Is it not also genocide when the peaceful Armenian inhabitants of Sumgait are killed? We do not think that the higher Soviet courts, than which only the Law itself is higher, have the professional, moral or human right to ignore our plea. Our hope is that the Truth will out.
>
> We insist on a court of sufficient competence to discover the truth. Surely the highest court authorities of our country should take an interest in this absolutely fundamental criminal act, which is what Sumgait represents. The High Court cannot refuse to establish and proclaim the truth.

Within several days, Akhmedov was sentenced to be shot, a

decision which aroused stormy protests in Baku. Meetings with the slogans 'Free Akhmedov' and 'Shame on Moscow' expressed dissatisfaction with the sentence of the Moscow court. Akhmedov's mother, E. Dzhafarova, issued a statement claiming that the real organizers of the crime were not in the dock and that her son had merely been a blind instrument in their hands. 'Shame' was cried at meetings in Erevan as well ...

As 7 November drew near – the anniversary of the October 1917 revolution – the Central Committee of the Armenian Communist Party was in continuous session. They were worrying about how the celebration processions would pass off; until this year there had been no problem. They distributed to district committees in advance ready-made banners, nominated marshals at places of work and those who were to carry the banners, and decided that at a pre-arranged time crowds of 'demonstrators' would file past the platform, where the governors of the republic would be standing frozen with their arms raised in salute, while powerful loudspeakers would broadcast taped cries of 'Hail to the working peasantry of Armenia. Hurrah!' at which another tape would issue an answering 'Hurrah!' Depending whether or not the Karabakh Committee decided to take part in the celebrations on 7 November, the Government might find itself standing alone on the platform with no procession to salute.

The Karabakh Committee was also discussing the forthcoming national holiday and what it was going to do about the march-past.

'Galya, you were in Erevan at the end of October, what was discussed at the meeting?' I asked Starovoitova.

'The whole thing started with the tune being played on the horn and the raised, clenched fists. These, together with the tricolour flags, had become a tradition. There was discussion about whether or not to take part in the procession. Then there was a report on the Sumgait trial. A member of the committee, Ambartsum Galstyan, was sending daily reports from Moscow. For instance, if there were not enough interpreters for the judges, then the meeting in Erevan would decide who to send up there. Then the meeting discussed help for Nagorny Karabakh.'

'The whole thing was a bit like a live newspaper?'

'Yes, except a newspaper doesn't take decisions. Speeches at the meeting can lead to immediate action. This meeting instructed two members of the committee, Levan Ter-Petrosyan and Vazgen Manukyan, to go and negotiate with the Central Committee of the Party about the conditions under which the people would be willing to take part in the march past on 7 November. "Go and bring us back their answer." Meanwhile, the meeting would get on with discussing other questions on the agenda, including a conference of 200,000 people by floodlight.'

Ter-Petrosyan was a particularly interesting member of the committee: born in Syria in 1945 and a year later repatriated with his parents to Armenia, he is a Doctor of Philology and the author of four monographs on Armenian-Syrian literary ties in the fourth and fifth centuries.

Ter-Petrosyan and Manukyan went along to the Central Committee, where they were received by Sarkisyan, the Prime Minister of the republic and the Party secretary for ideology, Galoyan. Ter-Petrosyan and Manukyan set out the people's conditions: immediate help for Karabakh in the form of vehicles and building materials. The representatives of the Central Committee agreed to send off a column of loaded trucks the following day. Ter-Petrosyan and Manukyan said, 'Good, we'll take part in the demonstration, but we won't be dictated to about the banners this year. The people will decide that for themselves; they are perfectly mature enough politically.'

The reason why vehicles and building materials in particular were asked for was because shortly before this bartering session took place on 5 November, the first secretary of the Azerbaijan Communist Party said in a speech that the inhabitants of Shusha in Karabakh, being mainly Azerbaijani, had long dreamed of building a bridge across the river which ran down a beautiful valley to enlarge Shusha. Quite frankly, a bridge was not necessary, nor would construction of a long, single-span bridge be a simple matter. The bridge, though, was a symbol intended to say in so many words that the other side of the river, which up to then had belonged to the Armenian community in Karabakh, was claimed by the inhabitants of Shusha.

This speech had electrified the Karabakh Armenians and their concern became known in Erevan, where, in the square, it was decided to make a symbolic outpost at Topkhana, a pretty, gently sloping spur of land. It was decided to build a small workshop there, where they could make some sort of household trifles. This little workshop was as unnecessary as the new bridge and was intended in the same way to mark territory.

On 6 November a convoy of vehicles carrying building materials duly set off for Karabakh, where, on 7 November, it was greeted with mass singing and dance tunes broadcast to an audience of deserted streets, stationary tanks, soldiers and banners proclaiming 'The Workers of Armenia Await A Decision'. This replaced the usual ceremonial procession, cancelled because of the curfew.

In Erevan the procession had not been cancelled, but it was awaited by the official party on the rostrum with some trepidation. The first column of marchers came through Lenin Square with banners in the usual way. The second column got as far as the rostrum and stopped. Tens of thousands of people poured into the square from neighbouring streets chanting *'Miatsum, miatsum'*. They tried to hoist banners reading 'Moscow + Baku = Sumgait', 'Don't stifle democracy' and 'Who ordered the soldiers to open fire?'

Everyone's eyes were on the rostrum. Someone called on everyone in the square to sit down, but it was cold and no one sat down. On the rostrum above them were the Party leaders, the Government of the Republic, generals, etc. In front of the appalled first secretary of the Central Committee, Suren Arutunyan, was a microphone, but he remained silent.

Below the rostrum there was another microphone belonging to the triumphant and happy members of the Karabakh Committee. The square full of people fell silent. Up to this microphone stepped Levan Ter-Petrosyan. He gave a speech in which he reminded the people of the help needed for Karabakh and of the

Sumgait trial, the problems of the democratization of society and environmental questions such as the need to close the Armenian atomic power station, which had been built in an earthquake zone, as well as various chemical factories which were poisoning the atmosphere ... Then he looked up to the rostrum and said: 'The Government must decide: is it with the people or not? If if is with the people, then stop obediently carrying out orders from the town with the ruby stars [on top of Moscow's Kremlin towers]. Use your heads. If you are not with the people, resign and make way for those who really care.'

Arutunyan was at such a loss that for a while he left the platform as if carrying out the wishes of the speaker. Before he came back, two other Committee members had a chance to speak from below the rostrum – Vazgen Manukyan and Ashot Manucharyan. Finally the first secretary of the Central Committee got a grip on himself and went to his microphone: 'Fellow countrymen, when, oh when will you at last be at one with your government ...'

But the people saw the change of meaning in his words and began to whistle. Arutunyan fell silent.

Levan Ter-Petrosyan was back at the microphone below again. This time he spoke in Russian: 'Respected comrades, generals, when will you understand at last that this is not Afghanistan but Soviet Armenia. Stop setting our soldiers against their own people. These soldiers are our own children. Should they turn their guns against their own fathers?'

In the silence which followed this remark, the horn player played his simple melody and the 'festivities' came to an end.

Meanwhile, tension was rising in Karabakh because of the decision to build a workshop at Topkhana to show that the Armenians of the Askeransky region owned the place and also because Vezirov had announced the bridge building project without previously obtaining Karabakh's consent.

Galya Starovoitova was in Shusha on the morning of 7 November: 'Shusha is in a very beautiful position and you can see Topkhana from the town, lying as if on the palm of your hand.

The previous evening there had been nothing there, just one rather spindly tree and some scrubby bushes. When I went there the following day with Valery, a nephew of Zori Balayan's, there were a couple of tractors and a builder's lorry, and they were already digging the foundations ... and Shusha was up in arms. We had a video camera with us. We narrowly escaped being thrown into the ravine.'

In Baku the news about Topkhana was greeted as a national tragedy: a sacred grove had been destroyed (although there was no 'grove' to speak of, as I saw for myself). The Armenians, it was claimed, were 'going to build an aluminium works', 'desecrate the landscape'. An atmosphere of hysteria erupted, based on inaccurate information about Topkhana.

The Government of the Republic forced the trucks to withdraw, taking the building materials with them, thus demonstrating they were masters in Karabakh. It was now clear even to the most passive Karabakh citizen that, without secession from Azerbaijan, there would be no radical economic or political reforms.

On 14 November a new series of strikes began in Karabakh, and an unusual dilemma arose for the troops deployed there. The strikers asked them to take away the Azerbaijani refugees in Shusha who were threatening the balance of nationalities in the region. These refugees were behaving more aggressively than the native (Karabakh) Azerbaijanis. Several phony refugees were spotted, who had left part of their family behind and come to swell the Azerbaijani faction in Karabakh.

It seemed as though, after Topkhana, a breaking point would suddenly be reached. Everything that had been building up was about to explode. The events coming on top of each other had set in motion a gigantic machine of growing national awareness, into whose great cogs were sucked thousands of people who had never before been conscious of participation in political life. In the past nobody in the corridors of power had worried about these people's opinions. They did not really have opinions. The will of the people, their aspirations and dreams were expressed in the decisions of congresses 'unanimously supported' by all members of the brotherly family of Soviet peoples. But now they had tasted freedom. And it had become apparent that they could not only express themselves of their own accord but also force the powers that be to do what they, the people, wanted.

Throughout the USSR there was a debate raging about the proposed amendments to the Constitution. In several places, the amendments – the right of a republic to make an independent decision about its disputed border – were more limited than they were previously. Stormy debates on the new constitutional proposals took place in Estonia, Latvia, and Lithuania, where the People's Fronts proclaimed their opposition to the new draft Constitution. In Georgia there were angry demonstrations; hundreds of students went on hunger strike for a week outside the Government building.

In Erevan, on 16 November, a meeting 200,000-strong decided to go for a complete rejection of the whole draft Constitution. It was also decided that there should be a national strike, no one in the city would go to work. If someone decided not to strike, however, he would not be molested by pickets, and strike breakers would not be beaten up.

Quite quietly, without any fuss, a wagonload of hay was tipped by the entrance gate to a factory, which meant 'Let the donkeys eat hay and go on working'. The next day, nobody at that factory turned up for work.

In Baku there were mass demonstrations and meetings protesting against the destruction of the 'sacred grove' in Topkhana and the construction of the 'aluminium works'. A whole series of newspapers, none of which had actually sent a reporter to Shusha, printed stories about the 'building threat to the surrounding countryside initiated by the Armenians', thus stirring up popular pro-Azerbaijani and anti-Armenian sentiments. Within a week anti-Armenian and anti-central government activity was to take on an alarming and dangerous form.

By 18 November the general strike was affecting all major Armenian cities. In Theatre Square in Erevan there was a meeting to demand changes to the Government's proposed amendments to the Constitution. Among those taking part was the President of Armenia, Voskanyan, and the Party Central Committee secretary for propaganda, Galoyan. The Karabakh movement, now a national one with its own deputies, acquired real power uniting opponents of the official authorities. It organized strikes and meetings which exerted influence on the decisions taken by the Government of the Republic.

On 22 November there was a session of the Supreme Soviet of Armenia in Erevan. The agenda for the day, apart from the normal items specifying the budget and the plan for 1989, included some non-standard items and at the end a review of progress on amendments to the Constitution.

Having reviewed the budget, the deputies turned to a theme which they had not discussed before: official recognition of the genocide of 1915. In this connection, they named 24 April as the official day of remembrance for victims of the massacre, declaring that day a public holiday, though the work lost was to be made up on another day.

The session was also to have confirmed the continuation of the struggle for unification with Karabakh, take a decision to close the atomic power station and, lastly, state its position *vis à vis* the amendments to the Constitution. (Hardly anyone doubted that the latter would be rejected.) But suddenly the session was interrupted by a speech from Arkady Volsky, representing the Central Committee of the CPSU, who was a guest at the meeting. He said that, according to his information, today, 22 November, was the start of bloody intercommunal strife. Armenians were being beaten up in Azerbaijan, in Armenia massacres of Azerbaijanis had already begun and the situation was already critical in Kirovakan. For this reason he suggested that the session should be concluded and members should return to their posts to start 'putting out fires'. He proposed that they should quickly accept the amendments and then disperse.

Some of the deputies agreed with him. But Ashot Manucharyan, the deputy from the Karabakh Committee, came to the platform and said: 'These are very important questions for our people. I suggest we adjourn the session for a short while. As soon as circumstances permit, we must meet again to consider the rest of the agenda.'

The session voted in favour, and adjourned.

It is possible that Volsky's speech had two purposes: the first, which he mentioned, was to warn of intercommunal pogroms; the second may have been to use the situation to get the session to reach a decision which suited Moscow.

The situation really was serious, though. Rail links between Baku and Erevan were broken and roadblocks had been set up. In border villages houses had been set alight and villagers attacked. In Nakhichevan the army had evacuated Armenian women and children. The menfolk at the risk of being burned alive had stayed behind to protect their homes. They too had to be forcibly removed and sent for their own safety to Armenia. An Azerbaijani mob had turned cars over and set them alight, then marched on the town Party soviet shouting, 'The Communists have sold out Karabakh to the Armenians.'

In Kirovabad a wild crowd had crossed the bridge dividing the Armenian from the Azerbaijani quarter of the town. Their way was blocked by soldiers once again unarmed, as in Sumgait. The mob stopped at their lines, throwing rocks and bottles, and screaming slogans. Suddenly the seething crowd parted and a driverless lorry crashed into the barriers dividing the troops from the crowd, killing three soldiers and an officer. At this, the mob instantly scattered in all directions. Attacks on Armenian houses began. All roads leading to the town were sealed off, while military helicopters tried to evacuate all the Armenians from the town.

In Baku, meetings of up to 800,000 were continuing. The demonstrators wanted the Armenian 'instigators' in the Government of Nagorny Karabakh put on trial, among them Academician Abel Agenbegyan, the writer Zori Balayan and the poetess Silva Kaputikyan.

On 23 November a curfew was imposed in Baku. Troops tried unsuccessfully to disperse the crowds; many thousands of people refused to leave the square, where camp fires were blazing. Attacks on Armenians and their homes became more numerous. There were attempts on the lives of Azerbaijanis. There were fatalities.

Martial law was declared in Kirovabad and Nakhichevan. Troops were put on active service alert. This meant they would respond to attacks with rifle fire. The stream of refugees in each direction from each republic increased.

Igor Muradyan, the founder of the Karabakh Committee, who had fallen from favour, arranged shuttle flights to Kirovabad, organizing evacuation and self-defence. (Later, he was arrested and sent to a Kirovabad prison where he was put in a cell with Azerbaijani prisoners.) The number of fatalities in Kirovabad rose, according to some sources, to forty, one third of whom were Azerbaijanis killed in clashes with the army. Nika Afanasyan told me later her story of how it started:

'We have lived all our lives in Kirovabad. We have a little house there with a garden. My grandfather and father were both born in Kirovabad. It all started on 20 November. The whole time they kept interrupting the television programmes with the news that the first secretary of the Communist Party of Azerbaijan was going to make an important announcement. The television announcer said it in such a way that we all thought war was going to be declared or something. We sat there waiting all day long. Then, in the evening, he came on with an appeal to Azerbaijanis to rally round. It all seemed very strange. At work on the Monday everyone was saying how there had been meetings and strikes in town. After lunch, a mob went to the Armenian quarter of town, broke windows and beat up a priest, Ter-Saak, and tore off his cross and returned to the town. The next day, Bagirli, the secretary of the city soviet of the Party, called for troops to come in. We thought things had quietened down, but the following day the crowd toppled the statue of Marshal Bagramyan (one of Stalin's leading military commanders in World War II), poured petrol over it and set it on fire. Then they dragged it through the streets behind a car. Then, when I was at work the next morning, I had a telephone call to say that my house had been smashed up. As I was leaving to go there – we live in the Azerbaijani quarter –

my boss said, "Go to the Armenian quarter or they'll kill you."
I went home and my neighbour came in and said, "Quick, they're
coming." And at that moment an explosive device was thrown
through the window. I was frightened by the smoke and ran out
and saw that they were attacking my father. I went up and said
to them in Azerbaijani, "What are you doing? If you want to kill
somebody, kill me instead." At this moment my Azerbaijani
neighbour was saying, "Nika, come in quickly and hide in my
cellar." We both hid there.

'After a little while they knocked on her door and said, "Have
you any Armenians in there?" "No," she said. Then they said to
her, "If you are hiding Armenians in there, we'll set fire to your
house." I thought, they'll set fire to it and felt sorry for her.
Another neighbour, a Jewish woman, took us in and she said,
"Call a troop car. Perhaps they'll come and get you out of here."
The soldiers came. "Get in quick," they said. The soldiers were
unarmed – they just had sappers' shovels. They took us to the
Armenian quarter – they had set up their headquarters in a church.
And we all lived in there for a few days.'

On 24 November a meeting of 500,000 in Theatre Square in
Erevan demanded the re-convening of the session of the Supreme
Soviet of Armenia. The Praesidium refused permission, but mess-
engers were sent to all corners of Armenia to persuade the deputies
to come and meet anyway. The people in the square were waiting
for the deputies to arrive and each one that came received a huge
ovation. There had to be 171 for a quorum, that is over half the
normal total number of 340. The army were surrounding the
administrative building and the other main buildings in the town.
Helicopters were circling continuously overhead. Evening came
and they were still a few deputies short of a quorum. The crowd
in the square waited anxiously. At last the final necessary member
arrived. General ecstasy. It was decided to hold the session then
and there in the Opera House.

'Was the President of the Republic there?' I asked Starovoitova.

'That isn't absolutely necessary. The Vice-President, Ganayan, was there – he had presided over the previous session. All the norms were complied with. Two independent deputies, Khachik Stamboltsyan and Ashot Manucharyan, announced the agenda for the session in their speeches. The crowd in the streets awaited decisions. Not long before midnight, the local television programme was interrupted and it was announced that a state of emergency was going to be declared, although there was no disorder or clashes of an ethnic or any other variety. The session concluded its work during the night, taking all the decisions postponed from the previous session. By that time, tanks and troops had been brought in to the centre of town. There was no way that people could disperse before the curfew. One of the deputies asked everyone to squeeze up tight in the square to allow room for people to get in off the dark side streets for safety.

'Later people began to disperse in groups to their homes. Those who were not in a group were beaten by soldiers with truncheons. The Praesidium of the Supreme Soviet of Armenia did not recognize the session as lawful on the grounds that it had taken place "with a disregard for proper procedure".'

There were ten days to go before 7 December, when the earthquake struck. The situation in the republics continued to hot up. Here is a timetable of events. It shows that things were building up to a great tragedy.

27-28 November
In Baku, during the night of 27 to 28 November, 10,000 people gathered in Lenin Square: 867 people were arrested, 18 of whom were detained for further questioning, and two offensive weapons were confiscated. The inhabitants of the town were disregarding the curfew. Several people were arrested for distributing leaflets of an anti-Soviet and nationalistic character. There were instances of attempted sabotage at oil installations.

29 November
By day the situation in Baku was peaceful. Several people received

threats in the form of anonymous telephone calls, letters or graffiti scrawled on their flats or houses. During the night, 695 people were arrested, 133 vehicles stopped and 22 people detained in police custody for breaking the law. Throughout the town rumours spread again that building was going on in Topkhana. The military commander of Baku described it as a provocation.

In Erevan 52 industrial concerns were shut down, 61 were partly closed. In Armenia as a whole, 161 workplaces were shut and 123 partly shut.

30 November

In Armenia the situation remained tense. In certain settlements where there was a mixed Armenian-Azerbaijani population there were clashes, which resulted in casualties. During the night of 30 November in Erevan 286 people were stopped during the curfew for various offences, of whom five were detained for further questioning. 1,115 vehicles were stopped and searched, resulting in no further arrests or detentions. Three offensive weapons were confiscated. An intense movement of population continued, meanwhile, from Azerbaijan to Armenia and from Armenia to Azerbaijan. Up to 30 November, 30,907 refugees had arrived in Armenia. To enable markets in agricultural produce to continue entry to Erevan was allowed only to Government vehicles or private cars with special permits.

A special commission in Armenia was working flat out on the refugee problem. Armenians were leaving their homes so quickly that sometimes they had not even had time to take warm clothes with them. 1,800 flats were allocated for refugees in various parts of the republic. A fund was opened to help the refugees, for which 250,000 roubles were collected. Within the previous ten days more than 20,000 Azerbaijanis had arrived in Azerbaijan, bringing the total number of refugees from Armenia to over 30,000.

In Nakhichevan, Kirovabad and other towns, mass disorders were provoked by hooligans inflamed by nationalist slogans, and disorderly mobs carried out a series of offences. People were killed. An inquiry was undertaken by the investigative division of the Procurator's office. The founder-leader of the Krunk society and director of a building materials company in Stepanakert, Manucharov, was arrested.

In Baku, to contain situations which were beginning to threaten the lives of local inhabitants, troops fired warning shots on three occasions; there were no casualties. In all, during the night, there were 556 arrests, of whom 31 were detained in custody. Four firearms were confiscated and 11 offensive weapons. 61 cars were stopped and searched.

1 December
The situation in Armenia remained difficult. 2,412 people had been arrested altogether, of whom 32 had been detained for various breaches of the peace since a curfew had been imposed. Pamphlets were distributed round the town appealing to people to return to work and call off the strikes. Even during the curfew, several thousands had stayed out in Theatre Square in Erevan.

2 December
Because of the continuing tense situation in Armenia and Azerbaijan and the number of refugees arriving in each republic who had been forced to leave their permanent places of residence, the Council of Ministers of the USSR formed a Government commission to assist them.

In Baku and many other places in Azerbaijan there was a new wave of meetings and demonstrations. People came out on to the streets and squares to express their support for the decision to keep Nagorny Karabakh as a part of Azerbaijan. Certain people tried to smuggle arms and explosive devices into Lenin Square. In the railway station district a mob of 5,000 tried to beat up Armenians. This hooliganism was cut short. Troops fired warning shots in another five instances to maintain law and order. In Baku goods were illegally displayed for sale. 9 cars were stopped for carrying goods without proper documents: 481 kilos of meat and preserved meats, 350 kilos of cheese and 266 kilos of other produce were confiscated and given away to residential schools, children's homes and hospitals.

During the previous two days rumours had spread widely in

CONFLICT

connection with the Azerbaijani refugees from Armenia to the effect that there was a great number of severely wounded and dead Azerbaijanis left behind. It was particularly firmly believed that there were corpses with savagely mutilated faces with their ears and noses cut off. However, official figures show that at this time 17 people altogether had been treated in local Baku hospitals, of whom 3 were outpatients and 14 were hospitalized for treatment for a variety of injuries. Rumours of mutilations, cutting off noses and so on were shown to be provocations and lies.

Measures were taken by the Government of Azerbaijan together with the military governor of Baku to assist families from various places in Armenia. By now, the number of refugees from Armenia exceeded 78,000.

In the last days before the earthquake the situation in a number of places in Armenia had deteriorated sharply. A number of incidents of intercommunal violence occurred with severe, occasionally fatal results. There were many documented instances of mobs running amok. 110 people were charged with being involved in a total of 38 criminal incidents.

Azerbaijanis who had stayed on in their villages were being guarded by troops.

3 December

The Council of Ministers in Moscow announced that they were going to take special powers to ensure normal industrial working was resumed in Azerbaijan and Armenia. Round-the-clock protection was to be provided to all installations of national importance in both republics. Any deliberate or unjustified withdrawal of labour was not to be allowed. The situation in certain districts of Armenia gave rise to disquiet. In the villages of the Amasiisky district, mainly inhabited by Azerbaijanis, military posts were established. Tension was also felt by the population of the Kalinin district. Here, troops were carrying out patrols and guarding industrial undertakings.

The situation in Baku was characterized by increased threats by extremist groups of action against Armenians. In the town five Armenian flats were ransacked and windows in 8 houses broken, and three instances of arson were recorded.

The curfew patrols detained: three inhabitants of the Shaumyansky district for the unwarranted eviction of Armenians and for attempting to install refugee Azerbaijanis in their flats; and a supermarket lorry driver in the Nasiminsky district for beating up a woman and her children.

In the military hospital in Kirovabad 25 military personnel were admitted for treatment to injuries sustained during incidents of mob violence in Kirovabad. Their condition was satisfactory.

During the night of 5 December in Baku troops removed everyone gathered in Lenin Square. Simultaneously, a state of emergency was declared in 12 other districts of Azerbaijan and a curfew imposed.

At daybreak the following morning groups of excited citizens were observed calling on people not to go to work. The reason given for this was a rumour that on the previous evening, Sunday, weapons had been fired during the clearance of demonstrators from the square and people had been killed. The military commander of Baku announced that as a consequence of the great number of people gathered there, the square had become a 'focus of insanitary conditions'. This was why the decision had been taken to clear the people out, to clean it, hose it down and disinfect it. During the clearing of the square no weapons had been used. Rumours of casualties were provocations, aimed at destabilizing the situation still further.

The number of threats to Armenians still living in Baku had increased sharply in the form of aggressive and insulting behaviour towards them. Instances of assaults on Armenians in the streets or on public transport had not ceased, nor the seizing of their flats. For issuing threats and incitement against the Armenians, several inhabitants of Baku had had their telephones disconnected.

In order to keep the peace at night, troops were ordered to carry arms as a deterrent. One arsonist was arrested. According to the official report by the military commander of Erevan, a convoy of 26 vehicles arrived in Kirovakan with refugees from Azerbaijan.

From 11 p.m. a state of emergency was declared and a curfew imposed on 16 districts of Armenia.

6 December

Many complaints were received by the Soviet Government from workers in Azerbaijan and Armenia who had been sacked because of their nationality. The Central Committee and the Council of Ministers in Moscow announced that they required an immediate halt to this most serious violation of the constitutional rights of Soviet citizens. Managers of workplaces who allowed people to be sacked because of their ethnic origin would have to take personal responsibility, which would involve expulsion from the Party, removal from their post and, in some cases, prosecution.

In Baku, crowds of many thousands tried to get into Lenin Square. Hooligans began a fight. There were clashes between troops and people. The metro stations were blockaded and public transport came to a halt.

In an instrument factory in Baku a rumour spread that during the clearance of people from Lenin Square there had been a clash between demonstrators and soldiers in which 4 people had died and a number were wounded. A stormy meeting started. During this meeting, a woman worker spoke and said that she had seen the corpses with her own eyes. Shouts went up for a strike. A commission of inquiry was appointed to verify the 'facts about the bodies'. The rumours were not repeated.

In Baku, 225,000 roubles had been collected for the refugees from Armenia, of which only 25,000 roubles came from private individuals. Meanwhile, in Armenia, by 3 December the appeal in aid of refugees had reached 1,537,679 roubles, all contributed by workers' collectives and private individuals.

By that time, 23,000 families altogether had arrived in Azerbaijan. The Ministry for Internal Affairs, in cooperation with the army, organized an escort for the columns of refugees from Armenia. Sometimes, when they were unprotected, they were attacked, and some suffered from frostbite and even died on the journey through inaccessible mountain passes.

In Armenia the situation remained potentially explosive. Meetings were being held. Ethnically based crimes were committed in various districts, and there were further fatalities.

In Erevan the situation was returning to normal. All business places were working, schools and colleges were open and transport was working normally.

The Armenian Ministry of Health announced through the mass media that the long-range health forecast for December warned of geophysical threats to health on the 9th, 15th, 22nd, 24th and 30th of the month. It was recommended that in consultation with a doctor, people should choose their own methods of taking precautions on these days.

Part II

DISASTER

At 4 p.m. on 7 December 1988 I went into the office of my newspaper, *Literaturnaya Gazeta*. The canteen there is a kind of club; in any case, there is no other place where colleagues can swop incidental intelligence and news. True, there are two or three offices where you can go to get facts and hear opinions, but the canteen is where people congregate.

'There's been an earthquake in Armenia. Balayan's been trying to track you down on the telephone.'

'Yes, I know.'

This was a complete lie. I could not have known that he had been trying to get in touch with me, because I had been dodging here and there all over town. I said it to put my marker on the trip, even if such things are not decided in the canteen. The truth is that as soon as I heard about the disaster I made up my mind to cover the story. I only managed to get a ticket for a flight for the following morning. While I was wondering what to take with me, Zori Balayan rang.

'I'm expecting you,' he said, reasonably calmly. 'Everything here is a shambles. On top of all our other miseries this year, we have to have an earthquake.'

'I'm on my way, Zori! How many do you reckon are dead?'

'Tens of thousands. Leninakan, Spitak, Kirovakan – they're all gone. Villages, too. . . . Come down and see for yourself. Get here as quickly as you can.'

No one on our brilliantly well-informed, indispensable newspaper knew of the existence of special flights. Unbeknownst to me, several planes had already gone down to Erevan, one of them carrying Chazov, the Minister of Health, and a group of doctors. They also took with them medicines, blood and equipment assembled at random because no one in Moscow knew much at that early stage about the scale of the devastation and the number of victims.

It was the same in Erevan as in Moscow. They knew about the earthquake as soon as it hit. Houses shook, the earth cracked open, but the city managed to stay standing. Frightened people ran out into the streets. The wife of my friend, the commentator Armen Ovanesyan, felt the shock in their flat on the sixth floor. She ran to stand in the doorway, apparently the safest place to be, according to announcements made in previous years, and started to pray.

After the second tremor she decided that the end had come. But the building withstood the shock. She ran down the stairs and straight round to her mother's, and for the next two weeks she could not bring herself to go near her own home. And yet, in those first few hours in Erevan, they had no idea what a fearful tragedy had engulfed their long-suffering country.

It is half an hour from Erevan to Spitak by helicopter. However, the idea of flying over the region where readings showed the greatest force of the 'quake had struck did not occur to the locals in charge for quite a while. This was a foretaste of administrative idiocy to come.

The first group of people to react to the disaster, as far as I know, were the doctors. The unrest which had been going on, involving meetings of many thousands of people, had led Armenian doctors to form permanent teams which could be got together at an hour's notice, even if those doctors were not officially on call. Soviet first-aid services are usually abysmal, so the early appearance of twelve teams of doctors in the disaster area is a matter for congratulation. It was these doctors who, as soon as they arrived in Leninakan, found some way (there was no telephone connection with the outside world after the earthquake) to send back word from the airport, which had remained intact. They described the colossal scale of the disaster and said that their efforts to help were an insignificant drop in an ocean of grief and blood.

It was a full five hours after the earthquake struck that Erevan, and then the Soviet Union and the world as a whole learned the extent of the earthquake. But there was still not a single reliable line of communication to the scene of the tragedy.

I managed to obtain thirty rolls of film that night, packed my camera bags and went out to Moscow's Vnukovo airport while it was still dark. It was bitterly cold. During the night snow had fallen knee-deep and it was still falling. The snow-clearing machines were only just managing to keep one lane of the highway clear of snow. To add to my difficulties, someone had stolen my windscreen wipers overnight, and I had to drive using one hand to steer and with the other clearing the shroud of snow from my windscreen with a scraper.

All night the planes were grounded. At the airport, passengers piled up as fast as the snow outside. Many slept on benches, on kiosk counters or on the stairs, but the passengers for my flight were on their feet. I assume that some – a few – of them had got tickets because of the terrible news. The majority had obtained their tickets beforehand and had been setting off to Erevan without any idea that an earthquake had happened. But now they were all upset and frightened.

As soon as the runway was cleared, the Erevan-bound airbus Ilyushin-86 was cleared for takeoff first of all the waiting planes. Once we were on board, the stewardess gave out over the inter-com: 'Will any doctors please make their way to the pilot's cabin.' Women were fainting in their seats from their apprehension of the disaster. In a chain reaction, the people sitting next to them began to wail. Doctors went round, with some success, calming them down. By the time we touched down, everyone was quiet but tense. We flew over the Armenian atomic power station, which is not far from Erevan. People in the window seats looked down apprehensively. It looked undamaged. Thank God!

At the airport, Zori Balayan was waiting for me right at the foot of the steps with Armen Oganesyan and Armenia's most popular actor, Sos Sarkisyan.

'You don't mind if they come with us?' said Balayan. 'Sos knows everything and Armen knows everyone.' We made our way to the exit, not the one that most of the passengers were heading towards, but another one leading out of the private VIP lounge. Neither Balayan, Oganesyan nor Sarkisyan, least of all myself were VIPs. My companion's confidence rested in the extraordinary recognition and rights with which the people had invested them as a result of their writing and speaking the truth about the Karabakh question, and maintaining their independence from the Government line.

Soldiers wearing helmets and carrying machine-guns let us through without asking us to show any identification, and we came out into the square where a waiting crowd of young people immediately surrounded us.

'What do they want?' I asked.

'They are students wanting to fly down to the scene of the disaster.'

After a few minutes, Balayan re-emerged from the door of the VIP lounge and told the students that there would be a plane to take them down, and they should wait where they were. The young people had brought nothing with them except their bare hands. I remarked that this wasn't going to be much help.

'It is complete chaos down there. Let them go. Even bare hands will be of some use.'

On the streets of Erevan there was no sign of the earthquake, but there were signs of the recent, continuing political tension. There were tanks and armoured cars at every junction, and soldiers with machine-guns. This evidence of military occupation seemed totally at odds with the quiet, sunny day and even more with the awful events which had taken place only 100 kilometres or so away. Balayan said something in Armenian and Armen Ovanesyan pulled out a bit of paper with a red star on it: his permit to be out during the curfew.

'Oh, Lord,' said Sos Sarkisyan, 'what have the Armenian people done to offend Thee? An earthquake – this is the climax of an unheard-of year in the history of our people.'

Balayan agreed. 'We mustn't distinguish between the victims of the earthquake and those of Sumgait. They'll start trying to replace the Sumgait disaster with this new one, but we will not let them. 120,000 Armenian refugees from Azerbaijan need help, just as the homeless from Spitak and Leninakan do. We have no right to forget them. We'll have to go to the hotel first, but then on to the other airport, Eribuni. Armenian refugees from Azerbaijan have been waiting there for three days for coaches to take them to accommodation in Karabakh, but the coaches have been held up at the Azerbaijan border.'

The Armenia Hotel is on Lenin Square, the central square of Erevan. Every road entering the square was guarded by a tank. Soldiers were standing around, glancing idly from side to side. During the day people could walk freely in the square, but in the evening it would be deserted. Outwardly, everything was calm, although in the hotel one could already sense tension. Some people, rather formally dressed, were queuing at the reception desk. When they reached the counter, they gave their name, adding, 'Reservation from the Central Committee', 'Reservation from the Council of Ministers' or even more prestigious organizations.

Nevertheless, the atmosphere was like, let us say, a party congress or some other important official function. Welcoming smiles and worried glances were exchanged. I got the feeling that many of these people had not the faintest idea why they had come to Erevan, but, nevertheless, they were absolutely sure they were indispensable. Our bureaucrats' self-assurance is the product of our seventy-year history: they are our VIPs, they are the engine and the brain which set in motion the great mass of the people – dedicated to their ideals and guided by them, of course. The song 'But without me, without me, nothing would have been here to see' could be their signature tune. In truth, everything would get done more quickly and work much better without them. These people assessed the scale of the disaster not in terms of the actual human victims and physical destruction, but in terms of the number of managers brought in to deal with it. Judging by the fact that there were many high-ranking officials who did not even merit the honour of being billeted in the special government Hotel Razdan, which had been reserved on this occasion for even more high-ranking ones, the disaster was of an extent which fully merited their kind participation. It has to be said that the majority of these visitors as well as the local leaders of the governing elite proved to be completely useless and, indeed, positively harmful to the situation – just as they are in everyday life.

Friends had reserved me a luxurious room with a nice view of a tank. I hardly spent a minute in the room, because as soon as I had loaded a film in my camera and grabbed a spare roll, we were off in Armen's car to Eribuni airport, where the wounded from the earthquake zone were being flown in. There were hardly any militia on the streets and on the approach road to the airport there were none either. The traffic was being controlled by civilians in ordinary coats and jackets, and, for the most part, unshaven. These self-appointed traffic controllers looked determined and at the same time grief-stricken. At the turn-off to the airport, they were turning back casual arrivals to leave the road clear for the ambulances which were tearing towards us, one after another, with their headlights blazing.

'Look at the tempo of the operation,' said Balayan. 'It will soon be dark. How are they going to carry on working down at the scene of the disaster without lights?'

We pulled up outside the terminal building and pushed our way inside through the crowd. Every other second, people stopped Balayan, telling him something hotly in Armenian. They were obviously distressed, but none of them was wounded.

'These are also victims, but not of the earthquake. They left their homes in Azerbaijan for fear of another pogrom. They want to fly to Karabakh, where they have relatives, but there are no planes. Over there in Stepanakert, they don't want plane-loads from Erevan. The coaches from Karabakh that were meant to come and fetch them have been held up at the Azerbaijan border. These people have now been waiting here for three days.'

'Who stopped the coaches?'

'I don't know.'

We made our way purposefully to the office of the airport's chief administrator, Suran Bardanyan.

In his office we found a crowd of aircrew, who had flown helicopters from neighbouring regions of the Soviet Union. By the evening of 8 December there were fifty helicopters operating between Spitak, Leninakan and Erevan. Also in the administrator's office I met Sasha Bobylev, whom I had got to know at the time of the *Nakhimov* tragedy in September 1986. (Then, Bobylev had taken me in his helicopter for a symbolic search for survivors from the mid-ocean collision of a liner and a cargo ship. Everyone who could be, had been rescued by the morning after the night of the collision; 500 had drowned in the accident. In Novorossisk there were relatives of the dead who still held out hopes that they might somehow have survived and wanted the search to continue. The images of nineteenth-century paintings of shipwrecks had engendered faith that a survivor might somehow be found clinging to a spar of the mast or on a raft or a barrel. In order to pacify them, Sasha and I decided to make the flight. It was already clear that there would be no more survivors, but this search was for the sake of the living who were waiting on shore. We hovered above the waves in a helicopter not designed for marine work and made the occasional pass across the town, so that people could look up and say, 'They're still looking.')

'We choose some pretty cheerful rendezvous, don't we!' I now said to Sasha.

'So it seems. How many Pier 15s will there be here, I wonder?'

This question meant nothing to the other pilots, but for Bobylev and myself it conjured up an image of grief. This was the number of the pier packed with refrigerator lorries where piles of bodies from the shipwreck had been brought by the rescue boats for relatives to identify. Naked women, who looked just as though they were sleeping, caught by the catastrophe getting ready for bed, were dressed here in their wooden 'overcoats' and laid out for their relatives to identify them. I will never forget one woman, the only one in a whole family to have been saved, who had lost her children and husband in the night sea, finding them at Pier 15. She had entered the refrigerator lorry and, seeing their four coffins, had fallen to her knees crying, 'Oh Lord, why did you leave me alive? Why did you not take me. I do not wish to live. Why did you kill my children, but not me?'

She had crawled on her knees before their coffins, pouring out her unbearable anguish and then, lay down beside them, willing herself to die. But God was cruel, and she lived on with her fathomless grief.

There, by the sea, at Novorossisk, there had been 500 or so victims. How many thousands would there be here? How many tens of thousands?

The airfield was full of people. Night had suddenly fallen and the darkness was lit by the headlights of dozens of first-aid vehicles, mini-buses with the seats taken out – simply turned into vans and now waiting their turn in case there were not enough proper ambulances.

Helicopters were arriving as frequently as trains on the Moscow metro. At one point I saw six in the air simultaneously. Some were preparing to land, others were circling, while others were taking off. They were mainly civilian helicopters of the Mi-8 type or their military analogues, but there were also some bigger ones of the Mi-6 type, enormous, noisy machines which made a noise like banging a barrel with a metal stick. One helicopter came to a halt without stopping its rotors. The pilot opened his window and a man ran up to him from the crowd of waiting vehicles. They exchanged a few words and the man raised his hand: two fingers meant two cars needed, three fingers three cars and so on. With a squeal of tyres, the cars raced up to the helicopter and volunteers rushed towards the open door to carry out the injured. It would be impossible for me to describe all the survivors I saw that evening at the airport, just as it would be impossible for me to describe all the dead I was to see later. Why, I wonder, do we thirst for descriptions of tragedies which have not happened to us, to our nearest and dearest? What good does it do us to pore over dramatic pictures, to discover all the gory details of someone else's misfortune? Is it merely to awaken in us a feeling of sympathy and involvement with the victims or is it the survival within us of some primitive belief that the offering-up of sacrifices to the gods will protect our own lives from harm? I do not know. The cutting edge of pain becomes dulled, people grow hardened from an excess of grief. An instinctive morality takes different forms in different people: some feel responsibility and Christian guilt even for evil brought about by others, whilst others protect them-

DISASTER

selves with a pragmatic cynicism, distancing themselves instinc-
tively from others' grief in order to protect themselves from being
affected.

At the airport I did not see a single person who would not have
wanted to share in their fellows' suffering, but the following day,
I was to see some totally different reactions. They carried a little
girl off the helicopter. She was swathed in bloodstained dressings
and a man ran alongside the stretcher holding up a drip. Through
one narrow tube, life was flowing into her. Doctors in crumpled
overalls lifted the stretcher into an ambulance. The man handed
the drip over to a nurse. He tried to relax his hand, but he could
not move his fingers. They had been clamped around the drip for
more than two hours. He sat, exhausted, on the tarmac with his
head in his hands.

'Was that your daughter?'

He shook his head in reply.

'She was still alive,' I reassured him. 'I saw her open her eyes
in the ambulance.'

'No, that was not my child. Mine is dead. My wife too and two
other children. All of them. Dead.' he sobbed, 'All of them. I
haven't anyone left. I am alone in the world now. Why am I still
alive?'

'And the little girl, whose is she?'

'Nobody's. Everybody's. Armenian . . .'

I helped him up off the ground and led him towards the ambulances.

'No need for that. I'm fine,' the man said. 'Its just that I'm
dead inside.'

The helicopters were unloading old people, children, women
and men. From their ashen faces, covered in dust from collapsed
buildings, they stared indifferently up at the sky. Many of them
lay with their eyes closed as if they were dead. And of course
there were plenty of dead. With smashed skulls, splintered spines,
broken arms and legs, many of the injured died on their way to
hospital. Often no one knew their name or where they were from.
I ran up to one helicopter which was on its way to collect wounded
from Spitak.

'Please take me along.'

The pilot looked at me with red, sore eyes and said harshly, 'No. I can't take you. I don't know whether we'll be able to land in the stadium. Try again tomorrow morning. I've got to load up with water now. There's no water down there, no food, no coffins.'

'What's it like down there?'

'Its like the end of the world. I must go.'

The helicopter taxied over to load up with water.

Armen Oganesyan came up to me. 'Yuri, you won't get down there today. The crews don't know the route well enough yet. They won't take passengers at night. Also, with all your equipment you weigh 100 kilos. That's a lot of bread, water, clothes, or medicines, right?'

'Right,' I said and ran to the next helicopter. They were bringing out a little boy with a bandaged head and his leg in plaster, followed by an elderly woman on a stretcher.

'Can I come with you?' I asked the nurse in the ambulance.

'Yes, do.'

The woman was lying quietly. Then she said, as if she was continuing a normal conversation: 'My middle son is badly knocked about, but he is alive. My other son is dead, along with all his family. It was my youngest, David, who rescued me. He must have recognized the ring on my finger.'

Zhenya Saakyan was sitting in her office writing a report when suddenly everything fell in. She thought she had fainted; it never occurred to her that it might be an earthquake. Then she did lose consciousness. All that was left of her office was a heap of rubble and she was buried beneath it. Her left hand was the only part of her showing, and that was how David found her. 'I came round when I heard him shouting, "Mum, grab my hand." So I am alive.'

Outside the first town hospital we came to there was a tremendous jam of private cars: people were arriving to see if there was anything they could do to help.

In the reception area there was a silent crowd.

'Name,' shouted an unshaven individual.

'Zhenya Saakyan,' I replied.

Immediately the whole crowd began to pass the name around. Perhaps someone there was hoping to hear her name?

By the time that second day drew to a close more than 2,500 casualties had been admitted to hospitals in Erevan. It would have been impossible to cope with such a flood without the doctors who flew in to help from all over the Soviet Union and from abroad. Following the earthquake, blood was in desperately short supply. The whole adult population of Erevan, including the Armenian Minister of Health, Emil Gabrielyan, queued up to give blood. Blood was sent from Moscow, Leningrad, every town where there was an official donor centre with laboratories capable of screening blood for the Aids virus. Throughout, not a single sample of blood with the Aids virus was discovered.

The Ministry of Health was like a disturbed antheap. The basic task was to allocate doctors quickly to jobs and to provide medical supplies. There was a shortage of bandages and medicines, although supplies were flooding in. Many of the medicines which arrived from abroad were unfamiliar to Soviet doctors.

'What were the basic problems?' I asked Gabrielyan.

'Not enough doctors at the scene of the disaster and a lack of elementary knowledge of how to treat the wounded. Many people were buried in the rubble for twenty-four hours and longer. After that length of time, a limb without a supply of blood begins to decay. When rescuers pulled people out, freeing their limbs, their blood supply immediately became contaminated with the products of their decay. The kidneys cannot cope with ridding the blood of this sepsis, and the patient dies. There were cases where the doctor, before freeing the victim, carried out amputations on the spot.'

I mentioned to the Minister that I had met the director of a Leninakan textile factory who told me that it wasn't only doctors who had had to amputate limbs. At his factory the ceiling fell down and one of the heavy panels trapped a woman's arm. There was no lifting gear available and, even if there had been, there would have been no way of getting it into the factory. For the first few hours the woman screamed with pain, then she lay there groaning quietly. People gathered round trying to help, trying to give her water. Then she fell unconscious and seemed to be giving up the ghost. Night fell. Volodya realized that she was not going to last until morning. In the dusty nightmarish blackout, punctuated by cries for help from among the ruins, there were only a few doctors and there was not much point in hoping to find a surgeon. By the light of a small fire he swabbed the woman's arm with iodine, tied a tourniquet round her upper arm and, tempering an ordinary knife in the fire, severed the woman's arm at the elbow. When he had cut it off, he fainted himself. But they got the woman to hospital and she survived.

Hearing this story, the Minister said: 'Yes, in the first days, when they were most badly needed, we didn't have enough doctors. More than half the local medical workers were themselves killed in the earthquake. In Spitak alone, forty doctors and seventy-two nurses were killed.'

'How many doctors were involved in the rescue efforts?'

'About 1,000 Armenian doctors and about the same number from other cities throughout the Soviet Union, 10 Canadians, 15 British, 30 from the FRG, 70 Americans. Norway and Israel donated field hospitals. Thank God for their help.'

I went back to Eribuni airport. In the first-aid centre there were empty stretchers and a good-natured medical orderly sitting on a camp stool. Rafik Saakyan was a volunteer ambulance driver from Erevan. He wore a once-white overall over a nylon jacket, his crumpled cap was tilted over his eyes. For a while he sat there in silence, then he looked up and said almost ingratiatingly, 'Now there's just the two of us, tell me the truth. You're a journalist. You knew back there in Moscow that an earthquake was forecast didn't you?'

I was dumbstruck. 'What do you mean, we knew? Are you suggesting warnings were deliberately withheld?'

'Don't take on so, Mr Yuri. Its just that some people are saying that up there they got fed up with all those meetings about Karabakh, with all the unrest and that, and decided so to speak to teach us a lesson. Of course its nonsense, but you know people. They are looking for a reason. Why should so many disasters befall us?'

'Yes, but use some logic Rafik. Even if we assume such a dreadful wickedness, look at the number of people who have come here to help. Look at the effort the whole of the Soviet Union is making,' I said with a feeling quite alien to me.

'I agree with you, it would have been an expensive way to do it,' Rafik replied. 'On the other hand, people are upset and want to know the truth.'

People were indeed upset and, because of that, they snatched at every rumour eagerly, not so much because they believed them to be true but as information. On the morning of 8 December somebody said there would be a tremor more powerful than the one at Spitak and thousands believed it. Everyone came out of their houses and waited. A scientist had to go on television to explain that it is, as yet, impossible accurately to predict the occurrence of an earthquake.

'I didn't believe the rumour myself,' said Rafik. 'The one about Moscow knowing that there was going to be an earthquake. Nor do I believe the one about the Turks tunnelling under Leninakan and something exploding down there. But all the same I believe there is some kind of cover-up going on. It simply can't be the case that it is completely impossible to forecast an earthquake before it strikes.'

I agreed with my companion on that point, remembering a chat I once had with an astrophysicist friend who was concerned with forecasting possible future global cataclysms. Once a month Alik Chichelnitsky rings me and says, 'Write these dates down.' And he dictates dates when possible violent natural disasters could occur. Sometimes, when he has time, he calculates on a computer the approximate map references for anticipated disasters.

I met him after my article in *Liternaturnaya Gazeta* about the little-known meteorologist and astronomer Anatoly Dyakov, a member of the French Geographical Society, who was exiled to Siberia in 1934. There he set up a makeshift observatory with a small telescope and devoted himself to studying the influence of the sun's atmospheric disturbances on the Earth's weather. He discovered various reliable correspondences between them and typhoons, droughts and floods on Earth. With the persistence of one possessed, he used to send telegrams at his own expense to the Government, warning them of imminent natural disasters. Doubters remember with amazement his warnings from Siberia which were followed by sudden hurricanes that laid waste whole towns. To this very day Dyakov has received no official recognition, although he was the only scientist in the country to predict the devastating droughts of 1971–2. He did attract sufficient Government attention to have a telephone installed in his shack in the Siberian settlement of Temiratan in the Altai region so that Politburo members in charge of agriculture could ring him up and get a long-range forecast from him.

Chichelnitsky was familiar with Dyakov's work, which was based on research carried out by two Russian scientists Voleikov and Klossovsky, and he supported me in a dispute I had with the Soviet Committee for Hydrometeorology. He has also done research into the influence of the cosmos on the development of the Earth, and his calculations were more than just reading tea-leaves.

I usually forgot the dates which Chichelnitsky gave me, but, if something big happened in the way of a natural disaster underground or at sea, I would remember my friend and check his dates, and be amazed that a majority of his predictions coincided with the events.

On the evening of 7 December I rang Chichelnitsky and asked him whether he had predicted a possible catastrophe.

'I was away on an assignment for two months and so I couldn't do any forecasts, but strangely enough I am quite glad that I wasn't able to calculate a major disturbance like the Armenian earthquake.'

'Why is that Alik?'

'Because nobody would have believed me. They treat all attempts to do this sort of calculation with disbelief. Secondly, I would feel some kind of responsibility for the fact that my predictions had been ignored. I have evidence that the Academy of Sciences was warned. A scientist in Kiev who uses similar methods to my own sent a chart of powerful earthquakes to them, and the peak of probability was on 6–7 December in the Caucasus region. Moreover, I have reason to believe that the Armenian Government knew about this.'

'But can you lay the blame at any one particular door? Surely, no one in the world can carry out accurate short-term predictions?'

'No, they can't. But it is scarcely possible to have any pretensions to govern Armenia without an official programme to lessen the fatal consequences of earthquakes in such a faulty seismographic zone.'

'Is there such a programme anywhere in the world?'

'There has been one in the USA since 1984.'

We said goodbye, but, within an hour, Chichelnitsky rang me back and said, 'As soon as I got the news from Armenia, I started to do the calculations. Simply to check whether or not my system works. Will you believe me?'

'Yes.'

'I got 7 December, magnitude 7, that corresponds roughly to 10 or 11 points on the scale.'*

In an average year on Earth there are recorded 20 major and more than 100 minor but destructive earthquakes which cost 10–15,000 lives a year. But there are catastrophes of gigantic proportions. In 1923 in Japan an earthquake and subsequent fires killed 143,000 people. Hundreds of thousands died in China in 1976. There were 110,000 victims of the Ashkhabad earthquake in 1948. True, the Soviet Union only knew about these tremendous losses many years later. In Stalin's time, and in Khrushchev's and Brezhnev's, natural catastrophes were – to judge from the Soviet press – privileges granted only to bourgeois societies. Stalinism, which annihilated between 30 (Roy Medvedev's estimate) and 60 million people (Alexander Solzhenitsyn's figure) could not allow the blind force of nature to compete with him in the annihilation of innocents stakes. The right to destroy within the borders of the Soviet Union was reserved for our own repressive regime.

It seems to me that the string of catastrophes which have accompanied Gorbachev's era is in no way a sign of divine dis-

* See p. 193 for explanation of Soviet earthquake scale, which differs from Richter Scale.

approval. I think there are various reasons for the ghastly sequence of accidents and disasters: firstly, the exhaustion of the fabric of society, which is no longer in any condition to withstand the increased burdens placed upon it; secondly, total political and economic apathy, which has seized the country since the middle of the 1980s; thirdly, the inability of the bureaucratic machine to think the new *perestroika* way; fourthly, the low level of professionalism in every stratum of society, from the humble railway pointsman to the Minister of Transport; and, lastly, the incompetence and technological ignorance of the majority of those in charge. The results are: the Chernobyl tragedy, whose aftermath we shall long continue to feel; the collision of the steamship *Admiral Nakhimov* with a cargo vessel; the explosion of an arms dump near Arzamas; the railway catastrophe when passenger trains collided on the Moscow–Leningrad line; and many more recent accidents. Of course, an earthquake is not in the same category as these events, but the number of casualties would have been significantly less if the medical services, the quality of the buildings, the rescue services and the organization and liaison of transport – if all these factors which are within human control – had been better. Alas, one often gained the impression in Armenia that these were also at the mercy of some blind force of nature or, putting it bluntly, were in total disarray. For is it not a well-established fact that Armenia is in a zone of high seismological activity?

On a seismological map of the region, Leninakan is shown as belonging to a centre vulnerable to earthquakes up to the 8 point range, the rest of the region up to 7. On 7 December, these figures were proved wrong. I assume that the predicted 7–8 point earthquakes were specified by builders or the Government, since buildings designed to cope with tremors of 10 points cost significantly more than those capable of withstanding 8 points. In the event, many of them did not withstand even 6, but more of that later.

It is well known that the whole of Armenia is an active seismic zone. Tremors have occurred at various times and in various places. Between 851 AD and 893 AD the ancient capital of Armenia, the city of Dvin, was destroyed several times. It was because of this that the capital was moved to Ani. The strength of the tremors is estimated to have been 8–9 points. In 1679 an 8-point earthquake in Garni destroyed the classical Greek temple there. In 1926 in Leninakan a tremor of 8–9 points was recorded. In 1931 the Zangezurovsky earthquake registered 9 points on the scale. It might have been expected that these recurring events would have caused scientists and politicians to be on the alert. Alas, no.

I am sure that of the nearly 30,000 who died in this most recent earthquake only a fraction did so because of the blind fury of nature. Going back to the question of why have there been so many dramatic events in the past few years, I would like to suggest that the answer is that we have now started to read and write about them. Tragedies of the past, now revealed to the contemporary reader, add a sense of further depression when he looks at current events.

'OK Mr Yuri,' my companion continued, 'I accept that they didn't know about the earthquake in Moscow. But they knew about the atomic power station, didn't they? They knew they had built it in an earthquake zone, didn't they? Why did they do that?'

The atomic power station is about 30 kms from Erevan, where the tremor registered about 6 points. The newspapers did not print anything about this. There were no first-hand reports. We can only guess at what went on there.

At the airport I saw Balayan again. He had rung round everyone, including Arkady Volsky, the special representative from the Central Committee in Moscow in charge of Karabakh, trying to organize the exodus of refugees from Erevan to Stepanakert.

'Zori, tell me something about the atomic power station.'

He immediately exploded. 'How many times we wrote, begged, saying that the station should be closed down! We knew we'd have an earthquake one day.'

'Do we know whether the power station was affected by the earthquake?'

'Apparently it is OK, but that is today. Tomorrow maybe there'll be a second Chernobyl.'

'Can one telephone the director?'

'Migran Bartanyan. He's a friend of mine.'

That was good enough for me, even though half the population of Armenia seem to be friends of Balayan's.

Bartanyan said that the first tremor was not strong, not even like an earthquake, but the tremors got progressively more severe. The power station had been designed to withstand earthquakes of 8 points in severity. As soon as tremors reach 6-point strength, the emergency system is activated and the station automatically shuts itself down. The seismograph recorded 5·5 points as the strongest tremor. The average length of these tremors was 200 seconds. Then there were three tremors registering 3 points. The station was working at its rated capacity. Both reactors were producing 815 megawatts.

'Just imagine what sort of bomb that would be. Built to withstand only an 8-point earthquake a mere 100 kilometres away, and the quake registered more than 10. They should close it down. What are they thinking of?'

In the darkness of night the helicopters were flying less frequently, people disappeared from the streets, obeying the curfew, intercity telephone lines were dead – it was impossible to get through to Moscow from the hotel.

'Let's go and see the mayor.'

A tired man with sad eyes smoking American cigarettes was sitting in his wood-panelled office. Big shots in the Caucasus usually smoke Marlboro or Dunhills. 'A Government commission flew in today headed by Prime Minister Ryzhkov. Why aren't you with them?' the mayor asked us.

'We know what the Government commission will be told,' replied Balayan. 'For that matter, why aren't you over there yourself?'

They spoke to each other using the familiar '*ty*' (like the French '*tu*') because Eduard Avakyan was a friend of Balayan's and therefore a good guy.

'Everyone has to be at their post,' said the mayor, 'and I am in charge of making coffins.'

'How much damage was done in Erevan by the earthquake?' I asked him.

'1,060 houses are damaged in some way or another, but none are in danger of collapsing. The sewage system is damaged.'

'How many people have been left homeless, in your estimation?'

'I would think about 700,000 in the country.'

'Does that mean, you'll have to build accomodation for 700,000 in Armenia?'

'That's in the order of 12 million square metres of housing. If you reckon the Soviet Union as a whole can build at the rate of a million a year and, if no building is done in any other parts of the Soviet Union, it will take 12 years. And that's not counting schools, hospitals or offices. We can't do it on our own.'

'I would punish the people very severely who allowed those nine-storey blocks to be put up,' erupted Balayan. 'They turned little villages into suburbs so that they could add to their empires, to destroy the rural communities. It was all done regardless of the human cost. Why all these Government busybodies? People have lived for centuries on the land, cared for it, now they all want to pile into the cities. Half the population of Armenia lives in Erevan. Who is going to foster a love of their homeland? Armenians are scattered far and wide all over the world, but the dust of their ancestors is here and so are their hearts. Leninakan and Karabakh – they are the wellspring of our race ... I can't bear it,' Zori brushed away a tear. 'OK, Eduard's got work to do. Let's go.'

Back at the hotel, we met a large group of journalists we knew from all the Moscow newspapers.

'There's a press conference tomorrow at 10 a.m. at the Central Committee of the Communist Party of Armenia. They're going to explain what's going on,' we were told.

But by ten the following day I was in Spitak.

On the second floor of Erevan's Eribuni airport the VIP lounge had been taken over as one of many disaster control points, which had poor communications and knew nothing of what was going on in the towns that had been hit by the earthquake. Those in charge at the airport, who sat behind the desks, knew at best what was going on under their own noses. Everything was by guess and by God. The situation was in control of them, rather than the other way about.

It went without saying that ambulances were needed at the airport, but there were many more than necessary. In Erevan itself, the sick had no ambulance service because the ambulances were all standing idle at Eribuni, while people were dying in town for want of them.

The victims of the earthquake desperately needed bread, but the helicopters were being loaded up with the first things that came to hand. Three helicopters would take supplies to one place, while not a single one went to another.

In the little hall sat representatives of the Karabakh Committee. Their popularity gave them the necessary authority to control the distribution of food. In a spacious warehouse they were loading up parcels which had begun to flood in from all over the world. Helicopters came in to land.

'Where to?'

'To Spitak.'

'Can you take us?'

'Let's have you.'

We helped load boxes full of bread, big rounds of cheese, sausages, mineral water, bags of clothes. The helicopter rose heavily and set off in the direction of Aragats – a mountainous massif which separates the devastated area from the Ararat valley.

'Aragats saved Erevan,' shouted Zori above the noise of the rotor blades. I nodded, reaching for my camera. At that moment, a member of the Erevan ground crew travelling with us pulled a handle and the door swung open. We snatched hold of his seatbelt so he was not sucked out.

'Now there's going to be a row,' I muttered, but the navigator calmly slammed the door shut and said: 'If you start jumping out now, we won't be able to stop to pick up your corpses.'

I thought that he was joking, but later, when I recalled the incident, I realized that the navigator had seen so many dead and carried so many wounded, he was simply stating a fact.

'Go forward into the cockpit,' urged Balayan. 'Commander

Dmitri Agbashyan is my friend. We're approaching Spitak.'

The first thing I could see was a road beneath us with a three-kilometre-long line of cars. There were enormous piles of rubble swarming with people; then it struck me that these long lines of builders' rubble were streets. The concrete skeleton of a sugar factory, the panels knocked sideways. Several smoking houses, some at crazy angles, but still standing; several houses with collapsed roofs; roofs lying on the ground; the ramshackle towers of a grain elevator, also reduced to rubble. It was an unimaginable landscape, somehow symbolizing collapse. Suddenly we could see neat mounds of sand and orderly rectangular pits – an excavator was digging graves. I suddenly realized that this view from the air afforded the only sign of constructive activity.

The helicopter circled over the town and drew away – the landing pad was occupied, we would have to wait our turn. I went back into the hold. My fellow travellers were sitting there in silence. Balayan was ashen faced. Suddenly, he leaned towards me and said: 'Clever bastards! They know how to take control of a situation.'

I understood what he was getting at. The commission which Ryzhkov was heading was trailing after it a 'raft' of official personages who, no sooner had they landed on Armenian soil, felt themselves to be in charge, shoving aside the local leaders. For many of those who had come down here the catastrophe was an opportunity to stand out and display their talent for organization. Tomorrow even more of them would arrive.

At nine in the morning Gorbachev, who had interrupted his visit to the USA, where he had made a speech at the United Nations and held meetings with the previous and current Presidents, flew back to Moscow because of the earthquake. On 10 December he was expected to arrive in Armenia. However, Zori was not talking about Gorbachev or Ryzhkov, but about an episode which had happened half an hour before at Eribuni airport, while we were waiting for the helicopter to take us to Spitak. As on the previous evening, ambulance cars were collecting the flow of wounded, which continued unabated. An old man from a village near Spitak came up to me. He had been in

Erevan on business and didn't know whether his children were alive or dead, and had no way of getting back to find out.

'Give me your bag as if I was your assistant, then they won't throw me off the helicopter.'

While we were talking, something was going on. Alongside the group who were bringing in the wounded, another smaller group had appeared. Behind them stood a black official Chaika limousine. The core of the group comprised Shcherbina, the Deputy Prime Minister of the USSR who was in charge (and remains in charge) of the Chernobyl commission, Shalaev, the Chairman of VTSSPS (boss of the most powerful trade union), Lobov, the Deputy Chairman of the Council of Ministers of the RSFSR, and Sarkisyan, the President of Armenia. When I went up to them, a row was in full swing. Balayan was in the thick of it. He was passionately telling Sarkisyan (who had bloodshot eyes from the tension of recent days) that the refugees who had been camping out at the airport for the past nights were neither responsible for Sumgait nor the earthquake. At these words, Shalaev turned away, making it clear that this was not anything to do with him.

'They have no business to be going to Karabakh,' said Shcherbina, 'they will only aggravate the situation.'

'They were born there and have the right to return,' insisted Zori. 'They need coaches. Erevan is bursting at the seams. These people have been sleeping for eight days on the floor of the airport. Come and see.'

'But buses were sent from Stepanakert,' said Sarkisyan. 'Why didn't they arrive?'

'Because they were detained at the Azerbaijani frontier. The Azerbaijanis express their condolences and simultaneously indulge in sabotage.'

'Why are you saying this in the presence of outsiders?' asked Lobov. 'What kind of provocation is this? Everything will be sorted out without your help. . . .'

'Is that how you understand *glasnost*?' demanded Balayan.

'There are no outsiders here,' said Sarkisyan sharply. 'Allow me to decide on Armenian soil what can and cannot be said.

A victim of the earthquake is brought out of the wreckage.

OSITE) The earthquake damage is comparable to that of a one-megaton atom bomb.

E AND BELOW) Bodies lying in the street while rescuers frantically search for survivors.

(ABOVE) Poor construction standards leave rescuers burrowing like moles.

(OPPOSITE) In the stadium at Spitak parents find their dead children.

(ABOVE) A galvanized roof rests on rubble – all that remains of a house in Arevashi.

(OPPOSITE) Supplies get through; some food is even thrown away in the chaos.

(BELOW) A physics teacher, Emma Gubatyan, is mourned by her husband and two sons

Tented settlements (ABOVE) spring up in Stepanavan to house those made homeless from blocks like the one on the right.

Balayan is my friend and I trust him absolutely. Let us sort this out, Zori.'

It is interesting that it was, in fact, Lobov who was appointed a little while later second secretary of the Central Committee of the Communist Party of Armenia. The spiritual (if you can call it that) orientation of Shcherbina, Shalaev, Lobov and hundreds of other politicians is understandable: the urge to maintain peace in a multi-national state gave birth to a fetish about 'friendship between peoples'. The much parrotted word 'friendship' has ceased to carry any conviction in recent times, but the official powers that be have totally lost touch with their so-called friends.

On the evening of 8 December there was a short television report from the scene of the earthquake and an item twice as long from Baku about the 'fraternal assistance' that was being offered by Azerbaijan. This broadcast caused indignation in Armenia, the more so because the whole of Erevan already knew that a group of fanatics in Baku had celebrated news of the earthquake with singing and dancing. 'Allah be praised, He has punished the infidel', 'Hurrah for the earthquake', 'God is just, He knows who to punish' – banners with slogans such as these appeared in Azerbaijani streets and telegrams with this sort of message (as well as genuine expressions of sympathy) came through the post. Others scrawled insulting messages on the sides of lorries bringing equipment from Azerbaijan. All this gave rise in Armenia to a correspondingly unfriendly reaction: 'We don't want any help from Azerbaijan, thank you.' Not a single 'Turk', as their neighbours were nicknamed, would be allowed to join in the rescue effort. Nevertheless, I saw Azerbaijani lads working to clear obstructions at Spitak and Leninakan.

Our helicopter turned back towards Spitak. It hovered above the only landing place which was clear of rubble – the town stadium. The door was flung open. People ran from all directions towards the helicopter.

'Did you bring coffins? We need coffins. There is nothing to bury people in.'

'Have you brought food?'

'Water? Clothing?'

A chain was quickly formed. The helicopter, unloaded in five minutes, took on board a wounded man and several women in their dressing-gowns.

Oh, the stadium! There was life and death there all right. In one of the penalty areas a field hospital had been set up – two big canvas tents with generators next to them to provide electricity. Inside were doctors from the Voronezh medical institute. One of them, Viktor Lavrov, came out for a smoke. He had been operating for forty-eight hours without a break. Occasionally he could stretch out on a camp bed in the tent next door, then it was back to the operating table. There was no water. All he could do was change his gloves between operations. There was nowhere he could wash his hands. There were few dressings available, but they were managing to save some lives.

'It's a shambles,' he said sadly, 'total anarchy.'

'Have many people died?'

'A very great number. Look over there.'

I looked round, not quite knowing at first what he was pointing to. On the withered winter grass, from the corner of the other penalty area up to the touchline, lay bundles of some sort. A few people were picking their way through them. Then all at once I realized that they were corpses – hundreds of corpses swathed roughly with rags. They had been brought here from all over the town or, more correctly, from the place which once had been the town of Spitak. The bodies were blackened, covered with filthy dust. Many of them were unrecognizable – their faces were gone. I wandered through this heartbreaking morgue under the clear blue sky unable to lift my camera to photograph these desperate searchers. A woman who had also been wandering through the corpses in front of me fell on her knees in front of a stretcher and covered her face with her hands. Then, as if warding off an evil spell, she shook her head. She stood up and ran after a man in a cloak and they went back together to the stretcher. She knelt down again and, lifting the rags which covered the child's face, looked up at the man. He nodded silently, and a dreadful, soft keening, a wordless moan, froze everyone within earshot on the pitch. Until that moment they could hope. Now, hope was gone.

'Those are my neighbours,' said a man in a quilted Armenian jacket with torn out tufts of wadding. 'She and her husband were standing on the street, and they sent the little boy indoors for a shopping basket – they were going down to the shops. The house collapsed before their eyes. She was unable to speak. While they were looking for him, they wouldn't let her near the house in case she died from grief. I brought their little Aram here. Where else could I go? There were no coffins. I lifted him up from under a wall and brought him here. And he brought her. She still can't believe it ... Well, I must get back to get on with the search. Come with me. They've found a woman alive under the rubble – she's talking. In two or three hours we'll get her out.'

He walked away and then I caught sight of another man. Slowly he lifted a small white bundle from the ground and, putting it over his shoulder just like a live child, walked towards the perimeter running track. He was moving slowly and at every step the top of the bundle swung. When he got to the edge I saw the face of a little girl of about eight years of age. I could not stop. We continued our funeral progress across the stadium, he in front and me behind. He went as far as a concrete fence with the fatuous inscription 'Sport, peace, friendship – the guarantee of health', then he turned to the right and went up towards the cemetery.

Of all the pictures that I took, only one is really special. I saw an awful lot of the dead and the living in those days, and remember the occasional thing here and there, but that child on her father's shoulders made me cry for the first time.

I left the stadium. Trucks were trundling slowly along the street, empty ones and ones loaded with the remains of houses. At the junction there was a hold-up – a crane had got bogged down. The road was clogged with treacle running out of a wrecked sugar refinery and the crane's wheels had stuck in it. Strewn along the pavement were empty mineral water bottles, tins of fruit, the remains of food.

The offices of the district committee of the Party had collapsed, burying all the employees except first secretary Narik Muradyan, who was out at the time. Three of his sisters had died in the ruins. He was now going around the ruins, seeing the military commanders who had come with the troops to Spitak, trying to co-ordinate the rescue work.

In the ruins there was complete confusion. Nobody knew where to find equipment so they were working like moles, scrabbling with spades and picks, loading the rubble into baskets and saucepans. The situation threw up leaders who at each building somehow were co-ordinating the work. Perhaps there was a command HQ somewhere, but, if so, not a single man knew where it was. If a vehicle or a crane was needed, they went out on to the road and stopped the first one that came along. At the cry of, 'We've found someone alive here', the crane operator without hesitation would turn to the place indicated. They would check whether the person was alive or not, listening for a voice or a groan. At every building stood the surviving neighbours, explaining to the rescuers where they should search. Only a few men could search at a time, because there was very little room in the rubble. One or two volunteers would crawl through gaps and there, scraping away the rubble and broken bricks in the pitch darkness, would try to release anyone they found alive. The others stood above, awaiting the outcome.

Near the ruins, campfires were burning. Private cars would come by to take away the dead or the living. But there were fewer and fewer of the latter.

The collapsed structures did not leave many fissures because there was so little cement in the concrete – it had been pilfered from the construction sites. The steel reinforcements were often totally unwelded, just held together with wire; that was why the falling slabs collapsed into dust. People had built tombs for themselves and for others to live in. You only had to tie a hawser round and pull, and it broke up. Salvaged furniture stood on the pavements. On a table there might be crystal glasses completely intact, but beside it a car crushed like a leaf from which, after two days, they were still trying unsuccessfully to extricate the driver.

Further along the street was full of vehicles – private, military, lorries, pick-ups – all types of vehicles. There was no one directing traffic at the crossroads. A worried army general pushed past me, a big shot. It must certainly have been a novelty for him to have to force his way through a crowd on foot without a car – it was Govorov, commander of the civil defence troops. It was these very troops who in circumstances such as these should have been in charge, co-ordinating the rescue work. In every big workplace there is a representative of this organization, they are paid money out of state funds. On placards issued by the department they describe the gallant teams who, the day after a putative atom bomb explosion, will carry out decontamination work and rescue the civilian population.

The destruction wrought in the Armenian towns, according to Dr Andrei Sakharov, with whom I later flew to Spitak, could be compared to the aftermath of a one megaton atom bomb – without the radiation, it is true. But the home guard displayed a total incapacity to impose the most vestigial order even in these comparatively favourable circumstances, thus demonstrating their incompetence.

Spitak had a population of only 25,000, whereas Leninakan had one of 250,000; by Soviet standards these were small towns. Imagine what such a disaster would be like in a town of one million inhabitants. The mind boggles.

'We are taking the wounded and dead to the stadium,' Kozlov, a senior staff officer in the Armenian civil defence, told me. But they were not taking them; doctors were and passersby who had stopped to give a hand. In the first days troops were sent in to the disaster area, but they had neither equipment nor training in rescue work. In the first hours troops and officer cadets actively helped the local people. The army area commandant of Spitak, Lieutenant Colonel Novakovsky, covered in dust and with dark circles under his eyes said tiredly, as if for the twentieth time: 'We should make more effort to organize the work done by people coming in to help from other areas often badly equipped. Brigades from Razdan, Ashtaraksky and Aragatsky areas brought their picks and shovels with them. During the first night alone 700 people were brought to the very nearest Ashtaraksky hospital. From all the districts unaffected by the earthquake more and more equipment and supplies are flowing in. But the shocks were too strong, practically every dwelling and administrative building in the town has been damaged or destroyed and, unfortunately, the hopes for any who remain buried under the rubble are very slim.'

'Who were the first to come to the aid of the people of Spitak?'

'Officer cadets from the Omsk Militia High School. These young fellows from the MVD were here to keep law and order during the curfew, so there was no need for them to be brought in. They also suffered casualties.'

One of the officer cadets, Kamil Yumashev, told me, 'Our group of sixty was based in Spitak. We were living in the professional technical school hostel, on the third floor. At the moment when the walls began to shake, we were practically all in the television room. But I was on duty at the night-desk. There had been a few tremors the night before, but this was something completely different. I couldn't even cry out. I felt a sensation of falling and something hit me on the back – I had fallen from the third floor to the ground floor. I was buried nearly up to my waist, my whole body was squeezed and it was completely dark. My mind was working quite clearly. I tried somehow to free myself, but I only had partial use of my right arm. I got hold of some sort of beam and started to rock it, shouting out, 'Help, somebody, help.' It took an hour to dig me out – my fellow cadets, the lucky ones and some locals. It was only when they were carrying me to the helicopter that I realized what a heroic deed they had done. The whole of Spitak was in ruins with people beneath them, but they did not abandon us cadets, they came to our rescue. Perhaps I was one of a thousand saved. I will never forget those people. I wanted to see the New Year in at home in Bashkiria. I shall have to put my wedding off . . . But everything is going to be all right, isn't it? After all, I'm young and healthy.'

A bit further on there was a Zhiguli with its boot open. Two men in clean coats and boots were running the length of the queue of cars and offering big round flat loaves to the drivers.

'Eat up, brothers.'

'Where are you from?'

'From the next town, Ashtarak,' they replied.

'Where's the bread from?'

'We bought it ourselves and brought it over.'

Ahead of us by the bridge, which had miraculously remained intact, a siren began to wail. An army jeep was making its way along the pavement towards the bridge. Ahead of it, looking just like a pilot, walked a mustachioed colonel in a Caucasian fur hat.

'Murman!'

He looked round and we embraced. Two years before, when avalanches of snow had swept away some mountain villages in western Georgia, I had flown down from Moscow to report it and Murman Gognadze had helped me get to Svanetiya.

'Ah, God brings us together in sad times,' he said, 'I've been here with my signals section since the 8th. In Leninakan establishing communications has been difficult, but we've got it sorted out here. We're camped up above the town. There are a whole lot of us Georgians. The first column arrived at three in the morning of the 7th–8th of December. We brought tents, food, medicines, lifting gear, coffins.'

'You brought coffins?'

'We didn't bring enough, my friend. So many children have died. Out of ten schools, nine were destroyed. Yesterday we went over to dig out the technical school. The boys were all killed sitting there at their desks, each one at his place, forty boys in one class. They only dug nine out alive the next morning, they had been in the dining-room, and for some reason they were unharmed. If you need a car, take one. Come along with me and get one. I gave the spare wheel away to some poor Armenian bloke, and some petrol – it is more precious than gold dust round here.'

'Why did he need a spare wheel?'

'He had decided to take his children to Erevan. I couldn't refuse him. They had a family wedding here on 6 Dec. They all had a long lie-in the morning after. He didn't want to wake his son and his young wife early. Now they'll never wake. They dug them out in each other's arms.'

The village of Arevashi is very near Spitak, but not a single crane or a single rescue worker was in evidence. The countryside was deserted. Many houses were completely destroyed; only the

shiny square galvanized roofs lay on the ground for the houses
had literally dissolved in a cloud of dust. In fact, the houses had
collapsed and under the roofs was just a pile of rubble. The yards
were empty, there were neither animals nor people. 80,000 cows
and sheep perished in Armenian farmyards during the earthquake.

In several settlements people made something like eskimo
igloos with compressed bales of straw – they feared another earthquake. Even the houses which were left standing were unsafe and
might collapse at any moment.

Outside one house a dead woman was laid out on a table. Two
old women wept over her loudly wailing. To one side, by the
destroyed corner of the house, stood a man, and two small boys
a little further away. I got out of my car.

'Can I take a photograph of the old women?' I asked the man.

'What business is another's grief to you? No.'

'I'm sorry, brother,' I said, going back to the car, but then he
called out, 'Would you send me a copy?'

'I would.'

'Then take it for memory's sake. It's my wife Emma. And I'm
Valery Gubatyan and those are my two boys over there. She
worked at the school, she taught physics. . . . I had come home for
dinner. Suddenly, everything started to shake. I scooped up the
kids and jumped out of the window, taking the frame with me.
Then I ran to the school. There was no school, nothing but dust.
Where should I look for her? First of all I dug out the timetable,
it hung in the hallway – that at least I knew. And from the
timetable I found out where the physics class was being held.
That's how I found her with all the little children.'

He called his sons over. The boys clung to him, not wanting to
go near the table where their mother lay. Not yet understanding
what the matter was, I began to set up my camera and got them
all in the viewfinder. Valery with one hand drew the children to
him and with the other began to reveal the face of their dead
mother. 'No-o-o,' cried one boy, twisting round so that he could
not see his mother's face. 'No-o-o.'

I pressed the shutter, thinking 'To hell with this job'.

Valery escorted me back to my car. 'You know, the shepherds said that a few days ago they felt the earth rumbling beneath their feet. Also the water in the artesian wells got several degrees warmer. We thought what's it all mean? It meant Emma's death, as it turned out.'

In the first days after the earthquake the outside world seemed to be hypnotized by Spitak, Leninakan, Stepanavan and Kirovakan. Only these cities were mentioned, as if in the villages nearby everything was normal. Then the officials and media came to, and it was observed that fifty-eight villages had been completely destroyed and more than a hundred had been seriously damaged.

'Where have you flown in from?' An old man from a mountain village asked us the following day. 'Are there still some places left undamaged? Hasn't the whole world been destroyed?' It was a genuine question, without a trace of sarcasm. Many, especially the old, thought that the whole of Armenia had perished. 'No, it hasn't,' we reassured them. And they nodded in agreement, not questioning why, in that case, for up to seven days after the earthquake nobody had flown help to them who were starving. Nobody came to help them dig out their dead, since there were almost no survivors under the ruins.

I arrived at one house in time to see them digging out alive a woman from the cellar, it was the basement of a shop which had withstood the quake better than other buildings. When two men covered in dust pulled out Anait Abramyan, pale but unhurt, and her children rushed to her, helpers formed a ring and carried her to the car.

'What did you think about while you were underground?'

'About those they can't reach. I listened to the noise and they found me under ground by shouting. I was near the surface and I was sure I would be rescued, but I had enough time to imagine how people were dying in pockets that rescuers could not reach in time.'

Many in Spitak and Leninakan were not brought out alive. Most professional help came too late; those helpers that did arrive early on were all too few. Professional Soviet rescue workers and volunteers often arrived in Armenia later than their overseas colleagues, and their equipment was much inferior. In the Soviet Union there is no co-ordinated rescue service, although there are more natural catastrophes than in, for example, Italy, France, Great Britain, Poland, Austria, FRG and USA, whence specialists flew to Armenia equipped even with their own water supplies and transport.

However, let us continue our tour of hell.

Five men were carrying a crudely made coffin. Alongside ran a woman, wailing and crossing herself. Nearby, another woman was asking about something. I asked Armen Oganesyan, whom I had come across among the crowd on the street, to tell me what they were saying. 'Nothing special. "Where", they are asking, "where did you manage to lay your hands on the coffin?"'

The key phrase was 'lay your hands on'. People used to obtaining all necessities, not by buying them, but by hook or by crook, used such everyday terminology even in these extreme circumstances.

'That woman – the mother of the dead woman – is saying that coffins were brought to the stadium and there is a queue for them and they have now run out.'

A number of people had gathered amongst the ruins of a house next to which there was a placard, undamaged and still proclaiming the message 'Hurrah for the Communist Party of the Soviet Union'. Here on the ground floor of a residential house there had been a special childrens' music school. The keyboard of a piano separated from the rest of the instrument and a doll with a smashed head were the dumb symbols of the place. To begin with no one knew whether there was anyone alive in the ruins of the school, but on the third day after the earthquake people clearing up had heard voices. Three men had made a narrow tunnel and they were asking everyone awaiting the outcome of the operation to move away – any movement on the surface of the ground could prove fatal both for the rescuers and those awaiting rescue. But the spectators would not budge.

'They are desperate to see something positive happen,' explained a militiaman from Rostov whose mother had died in the house. He had stayed on to maintain order, spending the nights beside a nearby campfire.

I waited for three hours for the little girl everyone knew was underneath to be brought up to the surface. Mesrop Gasparyan, who had saved three on the first day, was supervising the work – that is, he would say to the crowd, 'We need a saw,' and within a few minutes or half an hour someone would bring a saw or some other tool taken from someone who could spare it.

'You see the entrance is very narrow and there's a lot of broken furniture down there. It's very difficult to get through.' Finally he nodded to me – 'Get your camera ready!'

A stretcher was brought to the site. The militiaman parted the crowd. An ambulance came up quickly to the rubble which had once been a house. Several men lay by the hole and at last pulled up a barefooted girl of about twelve in a white blouse and blue skirt. She covered her eyes with her hands.

'What is your name?' I asked her.

'Gayane,' she replied unexpectedly loudly. 'Please bandage my eyes, they hurt.'

The first-aid car, siren screaming, raced off.

Three men emerged from the rubble and shook off the dust: Zograt Oganesyan, Varuzhan Pashyan and Never Barsegyan – all from Sevan.

'The fourth saved today,' said Zograt.

'Is she OK?'

'Absolutely,' he smiled. 'Now we've got to find a searchlight and crane. Voices have been heard at the bazaar.'

'And what happens if you can't get hold of a light?'

'It's a poor lookout. Who knows whether they'll last out until morning.'

A searchlight could not be found. In the evening I ran into some speleologists from Moscow. Accustomed to field trips, they were preparing supper in their tent and beside them sat some friends of mine.

'Where else could they go for a meal? Nothing has been organized. We can't put up our sleeping accommodation, there's no room,' said Oleg Pankratev from Moscow.

'We'll find somewhere to sleep,' smiled Zagrat. 'But we want to eat. We haven't eaten anything since yesterday.'

In those early days after the earthquake the problem of water and food in Spitak and Leninakan became particularly acute. The inability of the powers-that-be to organize the work is understandable, although one does not want to excuse it entirely. Their real authority, deprived of slogans and fear, turned out to be nil. Besides, the organization of rescue work really was beyond them, given their lack of equipment and professionally trained workers. But they could at least have organized food. There was food to be had in the devastated area, but in this, as in every other matter which required the participation of the authorities, total chaos reigned. Vans carrying food stopped when they came across people. To begin with, people only took enough for their immediate needs, but as they came to realize that there was no proper system of distribution, they began to take as much as they could.

A lack of faith in what tomorrow might bring, and distrust in the information which they were given, led people to hoard food. There was plenty of bread available throughout the town. You could take a loaf, enough for several people, and then come across a van with some tastier rolls and throw away the loaf you already had into the gutter. It was not until day four after the earthquake that Armenian field kitchens appeared in Leninakan and soldiers began handing out free food to those who needed it.

Many journalists arrived by the night helicopter, swopping stories, especially about Spitak. I was the only one who had been up into the countryside, except for two others who had gone up to Nalband.

They told me that Nalband had disappeared more or less totally: all 670 houses were destroyed and about 500 people had died. They found a shack made out of bales of straw and plasterboard off-cuts in which huddled fifteen people from various families. No one much wanted to talk, but one, a welder, told them that he was just coming out of the boiler-room of the house of culture when he felt the shock. His first thought was his mother. She was planning to make some bread, which meant she would be at home. He ran through the dust of collapsed buildings to his house.

Everything was gone. Luckily, his wife and mother had been in a lightly built kitchen; they were both covered in blood and had been buried, but were alive. He dragged both women from the ruins. Then suddenly his wife cried, 'Alik, the children, quick the school!'

They rushed over to the school and found some of the other parents already there. They started to dig, so far as there was any digging to be done, considering that from two schools there was barely a pile of panels and beams left. In three days they managed to extricate about twenty children from the 300 who had been in the buildings. Alik recognized his son by the watch on his left wrist. The child was buried, but his arm was showing – it was warm. 'Valerik, Mummy and I are here,' shouted his father.

'I'm thirsty, it's hot,' replied his son from under the rubble. Alik and his wife began to scrabble with their bare hands among the shards of window glass and slates, it was slow work. When at last they finally lifted the child out, they realized that it was too late. But even if they had dug him out alive, there was no medical help in the village for three days. How many died from a lack of medicines and doctors in the villages is impossible to estimate.

People began to worry about how long help would take to arrive. Winter was nearly here. How long would they survive? These places are used to thirty degrees of frost. Nalband is only about ten kilometres from Spitak. Even so, no helping hands had arrived from that direction, though on the first day after the earthquake some cars had come from Georgia bringing tents, food and clothing.

I heard much gratitude in many places for these neighbours, the Georgians, who had quickly and without fuss brought exactly what was most urgently needed. Apart from food and clothing, to Spitak alone they brought 120 excavators, 82 cranes, 4 generators, water tankers – all with drivers for round-the-clock work.

Benighted Spitak, with its blazing campfires, its heroic rescue efforts by helpers from various countries, its muddle, tragedies and occasional happy discoveries sailed on in the nocturnal darkness. I do not think that there will be another town built on this spot. It is impossible to describe the extent of the utter devastation at Spitak.

In the town there was a growing fear of epidemics. Doctors were not so much disturbed by the possible poisoning of food-stuffs which could quickly be localized, as the possible con-tamination of the water supplies. The sewage system and mains had been broken as a result of the earth tremors. The mains water was undrinkable, there were no bathhouses and, if that went on for too long, there would be a risk of typhus and lice. Thousands of livestock had died in the area. If they were not buried quickly, an epidemic could break out. Hundreds and thousands of 'ifs' had to be foreseen – and they were foreseen, but often on a purely amateur level. Professional planning was needed. Willingness was not enough, good intentions and ready helpers were not enough – what was needed was know-how. There was not enough of that, especially in the field of organization. It seemed as though the bureaucrats did not know how to do anything and above all were incapable of organization.

Gorbachev's visit was eagerly awaited in Armenia, where days of mourning had been announced.

If my memory serves me right, days of mourning in the Soviet Union have been announced in recent years only in connection with the death of a political figure of the highest rank. Usually the sad news is not announced immediately after the death, some-times not even on the same day. Nevertheless, the general public has quite quickly been able to work out the signs, allowing them to suspect something was wrong with a leader of the Government. To start with the hero in question disappears from television screens, ceases to be seen receiving foreign dignitaries. Then he enters into a lively correspondence in the newspapers. He sends many greetings and messages to the people or to some professional gathering or other. This would signify illness. Sometimes in order to reassure the people that everything at the top was fine, he would be allowed to appear on the screen in an undemanding role. Chernenko, for example, was shown voting in the usual elections, although the ballot box was not situated in the voting station but in a hastily camouflaged corner of the Kremlin hospital. He even said feebly, 'Good', meaning we know not what. For whom was this 'good'? That also is not known.

The public, which has been prepared by these indirect symptoms of a serious illness at the top, turn on their radios in the morning and, instead of the usual jolly music, they hear the strains of classical pieces, without any announcements, they know its over – prepare for national mourning. It does not seem to matter that quite often not only the general public but also those taking part in the funeral know that the deceased brought about as much bad as he did good, if not more – no matter what, national mourning will be declared.

A natural disaster or catastrophe, costing hundreds of lives, had never before been the cause of official mourning. Even the deaths of 500 passengers on the ss *Admiral Nakhimov* did not merit this observance. Because of the Armenian earthquake, flags were flown at half mast throughout the Soviet Union. I assume that the visit of Gorbachev to the disaster area was not entirely unconnected with the announcement of national mourning.

He flew back from America on 9 December, and on the 10th they expected him in Erevan and in the earthquake area. I assumed that I would be able to attend the visit of Gorbachev to Leninakan, and because of that I returned by night helicopter from Spitak to the hotel in Erevan. On the morning of 10 December colleagues from other newspapers woke me and told me that the previous day at the Central Committee of the Communist Party of Armenia the journalists had been gathered together and given their instructions. In order that Gorbachev's bodyguards should not chuck anyone out by mistake, as a mark of reliability they had given out badges of delegates to the Armenian party conference to journalists. Anyone wearing one of these badges would be admitted to the official press party. Journalists with badges were invited to gather at Eribuni airport and wait. Quite a few gathered there, some of them all correct with their badges. Because I had only arrived late the night before, I had no badge. The organizer of the press party was an old friend who gave me his and led us all off to the VIP lounge which so often reappears in our story. There everyone was divided into groups. I was in the first group, thanks to my knowing the head of the press corps. After that everyone had to wait.

I had never before taken part in recording this sort of official visit or one of these official welcoming parties. Since there were so many pens and cameras available, I reckoned that the news of all this would reach the public without me. It would be only a general impression stripped of any personal contact, whereas the impressions and conversations I prefer to gather belong to me alone. After the first ten minutes or so of waiting, I decided that, no matter what, I had to go out on to the runway, get a seat in the first helicopter that arrived and then talk the pilot into putting down in Leninakan.

There was only one helicopter to be seen on the whole airfield and, apart from me, three other people were hurrying towards it: Zori Balayan, Armen Oganesyan and Sos Sarkisyan.

'Where are you bound?'

'To Stepanavan. None of the journalists has been there yet,' said Zori.

In the helicopter there were baskets of food and bales of clothing. Help was pouring into Erevan from all over the Soviet Union and from many other countries of the world. Kind people collected things, packed them up and sent them off to Armenia, but some of the goods and food never reached their destination. In that same airport VIP lounge within a few days I was to see on the table open piles of Czechoslovakian sausage and French grape juice, carefully covered with newspaper to hide them from prying eyes. It was rumoured that imported things could be found from aid packages in Moscow markets of dubious repute. Certain relief workers did not think it wrong to steal a skirt or blouse intended for the suffering victims. I myself saw a black Volga car, which officials use in our country, leaving the relief aid warehouse at the airport laden with baskets with foreign labels. I am not talking now about the thieves and villains who will also not be forgotten in our story, but about people who consider themselves honest Soviet citizens and, moreover, aspired to the role of organizers of the relief effort. Even to this day they do not consider that by using the food and clothing intended for the victims they were behaving amorally.

I cannot resist comparing such people with the criminals who were released from jail near Leninakan on trust to help in the search and rescue of their fellow countrymen. Only two of the prisoners stayed at liberty longer than they had been allowed. They all undertook rescue work and not one of them was caught stealing; on the contrary, one of the prisoners searching for his son found a hidden safe containing 30,000 roubles, which he handed in to the authorities.

'We were quarrying building stone when suddenly everything around jumped,' recalled a prisoner named Martirosyan. 'Then drivers came by interrupting one another, telling us how towns and villages had perished. There were many among us whose relations and friends lived in these places. They asked if they could go into town to find their relations and mourn their dead. The whole prison camp supported them.

'I climbed up into a guard tower – I no longer wanted to live, because my only son and my wife were in Leninakan, but nobody fired on me, and within a few minutes an MVD colonel, Kazaryan, appeared in the middle of the crowd and told us we would get leave.'

The prisoners trusted Kazaryan and dispersed, though he himself did not know how he was going to carry out his promise – there was a tremendous risk of looting in the towns without letting loose a lot of convicts! He signed leave passes and shouldered entire responsibility for his decision. In all 248 convicts were released from hard labour camps – only those who had relations living in the devastated areas. On 22 December 245 returned (among them 100 earlier than expected) and one more reappeared on 28 December. Two absconded.

Convict Leva Martirosyan, who had been sent down for the fourth time for hooliganism and had just over a fortnight to go before his release, obtained a five-day pass. His son, Araik, had just turned twenty-four and had told his father time after time his fiancée was good and kind, but the wedding would be postponed until Leva returned.... Leva does not remember how he ran the ten kilometres to Leninakan. There was no sign of his home – just a pile of rubble lying in the place he remembered from childhood. The neighbours said the woman was safe. Then Leva rushed to find his son. The school where Araik worked as a cook was open to the air with splintered sharp-edged remains of walls.

'Araik, it's your father,' shouted Leva, trying to reach the place where the kitchen had been. Then Leva met the storeman who worked with his son.

'Where is he?' was all the father could say.

'I don't know,' replied the other, 'look in the lift. A few minutes before the earthquake he was bringing up a barrow full of groceries.'

Two concrete blocks filled the lift shaft. Leva tried to reach the lift cage, but the way was blocked with debris. Martirosyan ran over to the headquarters for clearing up the earthquake ruins and begged them to give him a lifting crane. Not until the following day did he get the necessary machine, and then was able to penetrate through the hole it made into the shaft. He came across a pair of legs. He dragged behind him a lifeless body to the surface. Leva managed to find five more bodies and took them to their relatives. Martirosyan understood that he was not the only one looking for a son. On the fifth day Leva returned in despair to the prison camp; he had not found his son, but his leave was up. Four days later the body of his son was brought to the camp in a coffin.

'Of course,' recalled Kazaryan, 'there were many misgivings: people thought that recidivists would start to loot and make trouble once they were let loose. But, look at this list, not one of 246 did anything of the kind.'

In our loaded helicopter, the pilot set off from Erevan at low altitude.

'Let's put down in the village of Luisakhbor,' said Balayan to the co-pilot, Yura.

'If the visibility is good.' Nothing else worried him. In Armenian airspace, helicopters and aircraft made themselves at home with minimal interference from flight controllers, who were working under incredible pressure.

'Source of light' – that was what the village's name meant – was not expecting us. More accurately, they weren't expecting anybody. The pilots unloaded a few baskets of food and clothing, and, without stopping the engine, asked the men who ran up to organize the distribution.

We went up to an old man leaning against the fence of a destroyed house who was staring fixedly at the helicopter.

'Did many people die here, grandad?' asked Armen.

He seemed not to hear the question. Then he said quietly in Armenian: 'Where have you come from? Is there still somewhere left intact?'

We were silent.

Then he gestured towards the snow-covered mountains and said, 'They don't know up there that Armenia still exists.'

On the last day of 1988 I flew out of Eribuni airport and realized that helicopters had reached only forty-nine out of the fifty-eight totally devastated villages. Many of them could not be reached by helicopter in the winter; mists and the lack of landing strips made plane flights very difficult; the roads were blocked with snow; and volunteer rescuers who looked like recreational walkers or climbers were often arrested by army patrols. Because of the proximity of the Turkish border, they were apparently suspected of secretly planning to escape abroad.

Of course, the mountain people who were used to living a rougher life were able to dig out most of the living and the dead, but nothing could compensate for their lack of medical skill. And their houses were in ruins. You can't survive winter in the open in those parts.

There were instances where the inhabitants abandoned their villages and made their way down to the valleys. If you take into account that the tremors continued for several weeks, no help came to them, and they were without electricity or radio, you can see why people thought it was a global catastrophe. (The lack of radio may seem amazing until you realize that obtaining batteries for portable radios and torches is an as yet unsolved problem of our economy.) Aleksei Serebryannikov, a rescue worker, told me about an abandoned village found by some friends from Moscow university. Only four people remained of all the previous inhabitants: two adult men, an old man and a boy of about ten or twelve. All four had gone mad. They were living among the devastated houses in a shack made from bits of the collapsed buildings. Inside a primus stove was burning with a canister beside it. What they were eating, goodness only knows – probably remains of food from the houses. Why they had stayed behind is also a mystery, when the rest of the village had been abandoned.

The old man sat apathetically outside the shack staring at the mountains. The rescue team gave them clothing and food. He showed no reaction. Then, silently and without any apparent reason, the two men began to fight. The child took the canister and, also in silence, poured more fuel on the stove. And then he laughed loudly.

I did not witness this scene, but it haunts me. The bare, snowy mountains, one abandoned village. A mountain shack. An old man sitting beside it, staring into space, while two men silently wrestle and a boy shrieks with laughter. Why were they left? What happened to them after that? No one knows.

Vartanyan, the director of the Soviet psychiatric health centre, told me that one in every three of those rescued from under the rubble suffered serious mental breakdown. Many suffered panic attacks in confined spaces or feared another earthquake. The shaking of a building from a truck going by triggered depression. Almost all adults found it difficult at first to sleep. Children withstood their experience of being trapped underground better, but their memories were more deeply rooted and it was unlikely that they would ever rid themselves of them in later life.

The reaction of the old man in the village was typical. Where there was no information about what had happened, elderly people (what few of them there were, because in country places the principal victims were old people and children, who were indoors when the earthquake struck) thought that the earthquake had destroyed the whole world. A significant proportion of people thought when their houses collapsed around them that Armenia had been hit by an atom bomb. Some, when they heard rescue workers talking in foreign languages, came out with their hands up, as if they were being taken prisoner. Vartanyan, however, considers that the majority of psychoses will pass, although the fear of another earthquake will remain forever.

'Do you think that there will be an epidemic of suicides?'

'No, nothing like that, but many, realizing their loss, wonder whether to go on living, and there were some who tried to kill themselves, particularly in situations where they were left quite alone in the world. However, that tendency does not last long.'

'Others' misfortunes, especially when they are frequent, can irritate people instead of enlisting their sympathy. I don't think it's impossible that there are people for whom the Armenian tragedy will be the last straw in intercommunal tension. The rebuilding of the ruined towns will require building materials and workers, both of which are already in short supply. Building projects, even in other republics, may have to be postponed. People may begin to be embittered . . .', I speculated.

'That may well happen. It depends on the general mental health of society and that is something beyond the reach of our techniques.'

The public sympathy of the first few days did indeed turn to irritation. It was based on the general feeling that everyone was helping them, but nothing is ever enough for them. This feeling was wittingly or unwittingly helped by the events of 10 December. On that same day, when Gorbachev flew to Erevan and when my friends and I flew to Luisakhbiyur, Stepanavan and Leninakan, twenty-two people were arrested by the army for organizing a demonstration outside the Writers' Union, which had been turned into the headquarters of the Karabakh Committee for aid to the victims of the earthquake. Among those taken into custody were five leaders of Karabakh, who, according to V. Erin, the Deputy Minister of Internal Affairs, 'had offended the military'.

Erin told the TASS correspondent, who brought it to the attention of the whole of the USSR, that 'nowadays the leaders of Karabakh movement, seeking out the slips and lack of coordination unavoidable in such extreme circumstances, attempted to demonstrate to the workers of the republic that they were playing the leading part in the organization of the rescue work. In fact, having established their headquarters in the Writers' Union, they pestered the personnel in the medical establishments and spread all sorts of panic rumours which interfered with the efforts to organize effective help for the victims. The activists of the Karabakh movement raised an unworthy stink on behalf of the children and orphans who were to be sent out of the area to be fostered by non-Armenian families. Playing on peoples' most basic human feelings, the leaders of the Karabakh movement were trying to instil into the populace the provocative idea that the evacuation of children was part of some programme to resettle Armenians outside Armenia. For their part, the Karabakh activists, playing on nationalist emotions and sometimes also on other errors committed by the previous Government of the Republic, won a certain popularity with the masses. However, now that a great grief has fallen on the territory and people of Armenia, they have discredited themselves definitively by their extremist behaviour. The time has come to use both political and administrative powers to stop these intemperate adventurists.'

In the days that were to follow, the papers carried numerous editorials on the arrests. The demonstration had also aroused irritation because it had re-opened the question of Nagorny Karabakh. It was painful to people who had dropped urgent work to hasten out of the goodness of their hearts to the aid of the Armenians to hear that the leaders of an unofficial movement, at a time of crisis, instead of devoting themselves to rescue work were issuing statements to the effect that those genuine and not insignificant efforts which the rest of the Soviet Union were making were merely hypocrisy. Maybe someone said it in an unguarded moment; maybe it was not the opinion of all the leaders of the movement or, still less, the opinion of all the Armenian people, but it had been said. The bird had flown, as my friend Balayan likes to say, and, although the papers argued that they were renegades and extremists, a hidden shame for the ingrates was harboured by many.

Then, in the earliest and most painful days, the announcer on Moscow television expressed the conviction that many Soviet people would be ready, if necessary, to adopt orphaned Armenian children. People really did want to, but this kindly gesture was misconstrued in Erevan, where the devastated Armenians in a state of extreme despair interpreted it as a threat to deprive the nation of its heirs. Alas, neither members of the Karabakh movement nor any other representatives of the intelligentsia refuted this monstrous and unjust assumption. And yet one more stone was thereby added to the wall of growing wariness, even hostility.

We flew over Stepanavan: from the air, after Spitak and Luisakhbiyur, it looked as though it had completely escaped damage. We had hardly landed, however, before the helicopter was immediately surrounded by people.

'We aren't important, we're left out of the big relief effort. Of course, only a few have died here, about 100 people, but all the houses are unfit to live in. Come and see.'

The helicopter flew on to Spitak, leaving us in Stepanavan for a couple of hours.

Beside the landing pad, there was a tented settlement of medical personnel. Alongside a large van, there was a group of people who had brought in an expectant mother. (That evening, just as we took off, she gave birth to a little boy who was christened Armen.) In the hospital tent the flaps were slapping in the wind which whistled round the bunks where we were sitting drinking tea while we waited for a car.

'We haven't any wounded at the moment,' said the local doctor. 'We've got a breathing space, but we are afraid of an outbreak of mass hysteria. People won't go back into their houses. They are spending the night out by campfires or in the temporary shelters which they have put together out of plywood and blankets. We need tents.'

It was a quiet spa town. Beside it is a wooded massif, a rarity in Armenia. Four-storey houses on the outskirts had collapsed in places. Sos Sarkisyan came from Stepanavan and he went to look at the house where he was born, only to find it gone. Behind neat picket fences stood houses with fallen-in roofs, cracked walls and crumbling corners.

It was quiet and warm. In this pleasant comfortable town the presence of tanks and troop carriers looked particularly out of place and stupid, but later events proved otherwise.

Heroic and dramatic instances of human goodness occurred side by side with shocking examples of human nature. A man came up to a group of rescuers and, when he realized that they had finished getting out bodies, asked them to climb up into the debris of his flat where he said he thought there must be a dead man. Without asking for an explanation as to why there should be a dead body in his flat, the exhausted rescuers scrambled up and shouted down to him that there was nobody there. Then he asked them, since they were now up there, to bring down his suitcase and his much-cherished imported blue pedestal lavatory. Cursing, they did so. When they got back down on the ground, he told them that the suitcase had contained 10,000 roubles from a car he had sold and then had the gall to claim half of it was missing, insinuating they had stolen it. His appalling behaviour might have resulted in manslaughter, which the exhausted and abused rescuers were ready to commit, had not the militia intervened.

After the first days, militiamen armed with Kalashnikov machine-guns stood in front of practically every house to deter looting. Any valuables or money the rescuers found were handed over to the militia for safekeeping. Armed Armenian patrols guarded the entrances and windows of shops. The danger of looting arose almost at once after the tragedy and sometimes state employed 'prospectors' took part in these 'tidying up' activities.

A rescue worker called Igor Pavlov told me that one day in Stepanavan he was awoken by automatic fire. It turned out the army was fighting the local militia. It had all started because soldiers had arrested two militiamen who were looting ruined houses. In revenge, other militiamen had caught three Armenian soldiers in the ruins and, although they found nothing on them, they debated, given the state of emergency, whether or not to shoot them on the spot. Meanwhile, friends of the three soldiers, hearing what had happened, got into their tanks and armed personnel carriers, and set off to rescue their pals. They succeeded, but crossfire ensued and the incident was only settled by bringing in a whole detachment of MVD officer cadets from Nizh-netagilskaya School.

On our flying visit to this normally sleepy town few people were around as the afternoon wore on. The only ones to be seen were in the small square in front of the Party's district committee headquarters, where army tents were pitched. An artillery colonel was trying to get through on the phone to Erevan to find out when tents and stoves would be provided as people were living on the streets. But there was no reply from Erevan.

Just then, a captain came out and said that a patrol had stopped two lorries loaded with tents on the highway. 'They had the destination "Erevan" written on their manifests.'

'The devil they have,' exclaimed the colonel. 'They'll take them all the way to Erevan and what hope will there be once they get there that they will send them back to us? Unload them.'

'They won't let us.'

'Arrest the drivers. Keep them here until you've finished unloading.'

Even I, a law-abiding citizen, could not find it within me to blame the colonel.

The helicopter was late returning and we began to worry that we might find ourselves stranded in Stepanavan. The absence of any flights was puzzling, for we had become used to a constant roar above our heads. Somebody suggested that the airways had been cleared in connection with Gorbachev's flight, in case there was a mid-air collision in such chaotic skies.

Sitting in the warm sun, I played back the tape of my interview with Minister of Health Emil Gabrielyan, in which he recalled his first visit to Leninakan on the night of 8 December. Only three days had passed, but it seemed a very long time ago.

You may recall that a team of doctors was sent to Leninakan immediately after the quake. At four in the morning Professor Ovanes Sarukhyan got in touch with Erevan and told them that they could not cope in Leninakan.

'I had to send a very large number of doctors,' said Gabrielyan. 'I had to get in touch with them somehow. I rang the second secretary of the Central Committee of the Communist Party of Armenia and asked him for permission to make an announcement on television and radio, and mobilize all doctors in the republic.'

(Note that in the case of Chernobyl the Minister of Health for the Ukraine did not make a statement until four days after the accident, after the *Izvestiya* correspondent Andrei Illesh had challenged him in his column to tell the truth, and even then the Minister lied.)

'I asked all medical staff to return to their work places. Within thirty minutes they were all in their hospitals and polyclinics. Drivers in the streets knew about my appeal and stopped to give the doctors a lift in to work. Within an hour of the appeal we were able to send over a hundred medical teams from Erevan.

'I made a second appeal to the public, asking them to donate blood. And immediately tens of thousands of volunteers surrounded the building of the Institute of Haematology and the hospitals where there were facilities for collecting blood. My third appeal was to ask people to go home, apologizing because we could not take blood from all those who had volunteered to give it.

'Simultaneously, we began to prepare for the arrival of the injured. By that evening, ten thousand beds had been prepared. All the skiving resident patients were sent home. Operating theatres were set up in all institutes, whether they were health centres or general hospitals.

'On his second call from Leninakan to Erevan Sarukhanyan said that all the hospitals there had been destroyed except one. It would only be possible to give first aid on site and then patients would have to be evacuated. I got on to Aeroflot and asked them to put all their resources into the evacuation of the wounded, which they did.

'The surviving hospital was one of old-fashioned construction and the authorities had wanted to close it when a new, modern, thousand-bed medical complex opened. But the new complex had collapsed in the earthquake, whereas the old hospital had withstood the shock. Beds were put up in the corridors and on the landings. They curtained off the operating area, and most of the amputations and other operations were performed there. Post-operative patients on stretchers were sent to Erevan.

'At 10 p.m. Evgeny Chazov, the Minister of Health of the USSR and I arrived in Leninakan in a plane loaded to the roof with stretchers. Other planes were bringing in doctors who had flown in from Moscow.

'Chazov and I got a lift in a passing car and went to the hospital, where the doctors were allotted to work. It turned out that some of them, about 800, were assigned to the district centre of Moralik, which had not suffered very much in the earthquake.

'Doctors from the Moscow Sklifosovsky Institute of first aid had set up a base in Maralik. Then they tried to get through to Spitak, but the roads were jammed with traffic. In Kirovakan there was less damage, but alas the hospital could not be used – the building was in too shaky a condition.'

Gabrielyan's short account added little to what I knew already, only it was noticeable that the Ministers of Health had been with the rescue teams on the 8th, but, owing to the traffic chaos, had been unable to get through to Spitak, where the organization of medical help would have been useful.

At 3 a.m. our pilots arrived at last to pick us up and told us the sad news: not far from the village of Nalband a military airplane had crashed. Bread and children's clothing had fallen out of the shattered fuselage, but the crew was alive. This was the first of three air crashes and the only one which resulted in no casualties.

Our helicopter set course for Leninakan, but we asked the pilots to fly over Kirovakan, where out of 180,000 inhabitants only 30,000 remained after the earthquake. The rest had left the city, in which not a single multi-storey building was left standing in a habitable condition. From the air I could see tents in courtyards and lifting cranes, although there were few ruined buildings.

In the devastated villages near Kirovakan one thing stood out: the peasants' houses had somehow survived, but the 'brave new' schools had become comradely tombs for the dead pupils.

We flew in a thick mist at low altitude over the railway track, which was blocked in many places by landslides and goods trains which had come off the rails. Eventually the line itself disappeared from view.

The arrival of our helicopter was only noticed after we had landed at Leninakan, and a frightened flight controller asked the pilot to move a hundred metres further on because we were right under the tail of the parked Tupolev 154 of General Secretary Mikhail Gorbachev. But, having moved about 50 metres, we stopped within the enclave reserved for the Government airliner.

No sooner had we emerged from the helicopter than a big Hungarian-made Ikarus bus drew up. Gorbachev was sitting in the front seat. He looked worried and sad, it was the face of a shaken man. He and his wife got out on to the tarmac, followed by Prime Minister Nikolai Ryzhkov, ministers and generals. They stopped by the companionway and had a long discussion before they finally mounted the steps and boarded the Tu-154. From an emotional point of view, this was probably one of the worst days for Gorbachev since he had taken office. There were no carefully planted passersby as are usually arranged by some local party secretary to protect his career when there is a visit by the First Citizen to his patch. Nor was Gorbachev taken along previously scrubbed and tidied streets, and the questions which he was asked for once required real decisions. In one of the streets his bus had stopped and a bystander, wishing to demonstrate the extent of the disaster that had befallen Leninakan, asked the crowd to stand back. Gorbachev's bodyguard, who saw what the bystander was pointing out before Gorbachev did, advised him to turn away, but he did look at the pavement where, next to a school, dozens of children's bodies were laid out in neat rows.

Tanks blocked the road to Leninakan. Afterwards many people told me that even on the day of the earthquake the curfew was not lifted and the tanks hindered traffic movements. Now, however, there was not and could not be a curfew because there were no houses left in Leninakan that people could go to – they were all destroyed. If there had been no control points on the roads, Leninakan would have been paralysed by the vehicles rushing in to help. Even so, there were too many for the few remaining streets.

My impression on that first visit was that not only had the town been destroyed but also the areas beyond. The town, filled with stench and dust, was sinking into chaos. People were sorting through the remains of furniture on enormous heaps of broken bricks and reinforced concrete. Cranes and excavators were helping them, brought in by airplanes from all over the country, and people from all over the U S S R were sitting behind the steering wheels of vehicles. Townspeople sat or squatted round campfires, huddled in blankets which had been thrown over them, waiting for the moment when those on the heaps of rubble would discover the body of a person who had been their father or their son or their husband. Then, when their relations had been found, they would get up and go to the coffin store.

Coffins of various sorts lay about everywhere: covered with black and red material, planed and made from chipboard, heavy or light, big or small, even tiny children's coffins. There had been coffins even on the second day, but now there were thousands of them on the streets and one quickly became used to them. The rescuers drank lemonade and would put their bottles down on a coffin or sat on one to take a breather. Coffins haunted your gaze wherever you looked. Trucks went along loaded with them, and they stuck out of the boots of private cars. (It was thus that thieves stole ownerless cars from Leninakan, for who would think of stopping a car with a coffin in the boot?)

We walked round the town on foot, Sos, Armen and I; Zori had gone back to Erevan. There was a traffic jam a kilometre long. There was a total lack of organization everywhere. An ambulance siren was going and drivers tried to pull over to let it by. At the level crossing over the railway, two men with lengths of metal tubing were beating the car bodies and windows of those blocking the route; they were practically in hysterics, because two ambulances were stuck in the stationery jam. An ambulance in Leninakan meant hope; it meant they were carrying someone who was still alive. But the problem was that they couldn't get them anywhere – they were stuck. So a blow on the bonnet, and an ambulance crawled out into the path of the oncoming traffic. No one objected. The blare of car hooters, the exhaust fumes, shouting.

The enormous building of the department store guarded by machine gunners was rickety. The ceilings had collapsed, burying hundreds of people. New blocks of flats were devastated, but alongside were three- and four-storey ones intact.

We emerged on to a boulevard. Soldiers were putting up tents, big tents, but so far without stoves. There were not enough stoves; factories were all ready to make them from pipes, but they had not got the pipes yet.

Night was falling fast. There was no electricity, only the occasional traffic lights which by some miracle were flashing alternately red and green. On benches there was bedding. The majority of survivors were afraid to go indoors. Many had managed to escape from the town leaving all their possessions behind in their flats. Leninakan by night was a town full of shadows and campfires, torches, the lighted ends of cigarettes.

The three of us walked on towards Lenin Square. In the gloom we could make out the statue. Monuments had survived. Several searchlights lit up the ruins near the Children's World department store. Some lads from Donetsk were putting a line round a concrete slab. By the light of a campfire I tried to photograph a man with a handsome, impassive face.

'See that chap over there, the one you tried to get a picture of? He's buried both his children and his wife. Now he's waiting for his aunt to be found,' said a woman bending towards me in a pink dressing-gown with a coat thrown over it.

'Did you live here too?'

'Yes. I'm waiting for them to find my husband,' she said matter-of-factly, just as if she were waiting for him to get home from work.

We wandered on through the town to the house of some friends of Armen. While he went to the entrance of a darkened three-storey building, Sos and I tried to stop a car to tell someone about a fire which apparently no one had noticed. There was a tank at the junction with a soldier sitting on top of it. We went over to him.

'Tell them on your radio that there's a fire.'

'I've told them, they're on their way.'

Shortly after the fire fighters arrived Armen came back radiant: his friends were alive, but not at home yet.

On the square stood a van with bread, which no one was taking. The streets were strewn with leftovers of food, just like Spitak. A little further on there was another van. Into outstretched hands Georgians were distributing cheese, packets of butter and sausages. Four days had gone by, but disorder and anarchy still reigned here. A long row of canisters bore witness that fuel was in short supply, and there were no public lavatories anywhere. On the other hand, some rudiments of organization could be observed: on the street where the army headquarters was situated patrols were not letting passersby through.

By the ruins of a nine-storey block of flats there was a portable electric generator and people crowded around. I pushed my way through to the lighted hole where three men were working.

'What have you got here?'

'Italian sniffer dogs detected some people alive. Now they've gone, we're trying to get them out.'

'Who's down there?'

'A woman on top of a little boy, but her daughter's dead and is lying there in front of her eyes. The woman's in a bad way. She probably has crush syndrome.'

I crawled to the edge of the hole. I could only see two heads: the dead girl and her mother. The boy was evidently further down.

'Don't get in our way. We still don't know whether we can save them. What the hell are you doing here with a camera?' asked a short, bewhiskered man with sunken eyes. I moved off to one side in some embarrassment.

They worked away for some time. Suddenly the motor stopped and the light went out. The onlookers, sitting on crates beside the campfire, became anxious. The rescue work continued by torchlight.

They pulled the woman out around midnight – she was unconscious. They carried her to a van. After her, they got the boy out. Evidently he asked for some water in Armenian, because at once several people rushed up to him with bottles, but the stern little man said quietly but firmly, 'Stay back!' and they all stopped.

Afterwards I sat by the fire with him and we had a smoke.

'I'm sorry I bit your head off back there. The strain was terrific. My name's Yuri Bukharin. I'm an intern from the Moscow Medical Institute.'

'Have you been busy?'

'Fiendishly. To begin with, we had to forage for medicines ourselves. We went to the maternity hospital and took all the supplies they had there.'

'What about the patients at the maternity hospital?'

He didn't reply immediately. He buried his head in his hands, and, as if he was stating the obvious, said angrily, 'The maternity hospital itself had collapsed. Sixty expectant mothers died. And newly born babies with their mothers and the doctors died and the nurses died. Oh, God, do you feel guilty that you're still alive?' Without waiting for an answer from me he said, 'I do.'

Campfires, everywhere there were campfires. People sat by the fires with the low, dusty sky above and smouldering rubble all around. In the dark car headlights twinkled and in places sparks flew. That meant they were cutting metal – someone was in luck.

Despite the darkness, I managed to get to the military headquarters. Downstairs there were armed guards and on the walls behind were lists of the dead, whenever their identity could be established. Next to these were lists naming surviving children, unharmed or wounded, and the names of adults in case someone might be inquiring after them. In this great wheel of life and death people could be lost even if they had survived. Later, in Erevan, on the walls of the Central Committee of the Komsomol (Communist Youth League) I saw lists of 70,000 missing persons. A group called Search helped 20,000 children in the space of ten days to find their relations. In Search young mathematicians,

By 19 December about 900 cranes and over 1,000 tipper lorries are working in the disaster area.

'Lenin is more alive today than anyone' says the slogan under his portrait (ABOVE), as bodies are lined up in front of his statue (LEFT).

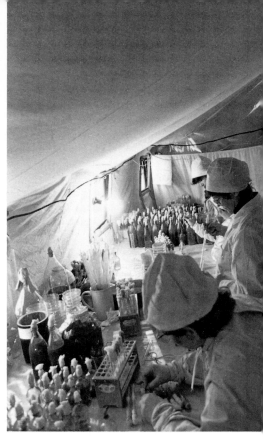

Trained sniffer dogs arrive late in the day as fears of an epidemic grow.

(OPPOSITE) Aftermath: furniture and identity documents lie in piles; some people queue for evacuation, while others make their own arrangements.

Dr Andrei Sakharov (LEFT) visits the scene of the earthquake, while tanks stand guard in Lenin Square, Erevan.

Time worn face of tragedy.

Yurts serving as medical stations in Dzhrashen.

The long wait begins – it will be many years before the people can rebuild their cities and their lives.

cyberneticists and computer programmers joined forces to establish a computer network where special search groups entered their information.

Sambel Garbyan, a man with an extraordinary memory, helped many lost persons. This twenty-six-year-old lawyer committed to memory thousands of names and addresses and could instantly tell them to relatives. This human computer reunited hundreds of families.

Details of people who had volunteered to take an orphaned child were also kept here at Search. There were about 10,000 volunteer families, but for the time being not a single child had been handed over. In Armenia, family ties are very strong. It is considered the duty of even the most distant relatives to take in a child in need, which is fine if such relatives exist.

Children who were orphaned before the earthquake were also suffering. Cheated again by fate, many of them were now wounded or mutilated in the earthquake. Homes for the deaf and blind were destroyed as were homes for the elderly. Against the background of such enormous devastation such unfortunate individuals risked being overlooked, although a Politburo committee promised to build everything that was needed for the Ministry of Social Security. In Leninakan there were no computerized lists as yet. The majority of names were written by hand beside a photograph of the missing person.

On the ground floor of the temporary military HQ, on the staircase and along the first-floor corridor builders and fitters had gathered from all over the Soviet Union. Every day the Government committee held hearings here in a small hall with a tiny stage packed with heads of ministries or building firms and generals.

'60,000 men are taking part in clearing the rubble,' announced an official from Shcherbina's staff.

I enquired where they were sleeping and how they were being fed. On the streets, in cold unheated tents and in cars was the reply, and they were eating whatever someone might bring along, what they could forage for themselves. The big firms, however, were beginning to organize canteens.

At the school there was more light than in other places; one searchlight had been provided by the army, the other by a French rescue team. Of the two school buildings, the old one and the new, only the old one had survived. Nobody knew how many children and teachers were still trapped in the ruins of the new one. It was only known that at the time of the earthquake there had been a total of 1,000 people in both buildings. Rescue work had been going on for three days now. They had succeeded in digging out three hundred children and adults, only a few of them alive. The French were greeted as a last hope. They were hoping for miracles from the sniffer dogs and equipment.

'Let's wait here,' said Sos, 'I've a feeling they might find someone alive.'

A black French rescue worker, who had particularly attracted the attention of Leninakaners, sent a sheepdog into the ruins. It went to the place where they had just been digging, turned round and ran off, came back, then ran off again and lay down. A combined Soviet and French team made a hole with a crowbar and let down into it a sensitive miniature microphone capable of picking up even faint breathing or heartbeats.

'Nothing,' shouted the man with the crowbar.

The Frenchman put on the earphones and listened for a sound. Nothing. They tried in another place, but still there was silence. Sos had been wrong, but in the morning we heard that under the concrete slab where the dog had lain they had found a whole class of dead children.

If only there had been dogs and equipment on the first day. If only we had a rescue service like every other self-respecting country. If only they had got hold of our volunteer rescue workers and our climbers and cavers in time....

Armen suggested we stay the night with his friends who had survived.

Until that evening, the Muradyan family, of whose luck I spoke at the beginning of my book, had been living in their garage. Their block had remained standing, although the walls between the rooms in the neighbouring flats on the first and second floors had collapsed. Their neighbours had locked up their flats and gone away, but the Muradyan's had remained. Their flat on the fourth floor was hardly damaged, but they were afraid to go back inside in case one of the recurrent tremors (there had been 150 in the past few days) brought the rest of the house down round their ears.

'What a town this was,' exclaimed Armen, 'hospitable, prosperous, generous. Even at a time like this, look what they have set out for us.'

On the table there was brandy and vodka. There was cheesecake, *khachapuri* (a sort of local pizza), roast pork, home-made pickles, cheese and sausage.

'I'm sorry there won't be a hot course. I haven't got a stove and water is terribly short,' said Olga, the one who ran out of the collapsing block of flats on 7 December. 'But Aunt Sonya will make us some coffee. We'll find enough water for that.'

By candlelight we sat and talked about the future of Leninakan. We agreed that many people would never come back, fear would prevail over attachment to place; it would be necessary to build a beautiful city of two- and three-storey houses only.

'In England Mrs Thatcher said that three-quarters of the population now own their own homes,' said Olga's husband, Razmik. 'In Australia they all live in bungalows, in America too. Only banks and companies have skyscrapers. We have no banks, and "companies" try to hide themselves underground.'

'No,' observed a worker from the district committee of the Party, who had been silent up till then, 'we haven't enough room for that sort of building. We can build up to five storeys, but they must be well built. The high-rise Shirak motel is still standing, it didn't collapse. In Japan they build skyscrapers designed to withstand earthquakes.'

'We don't need skyscrapers,' said Sos Sarkisyan. 'Armenians like living with their feet on the ground. Let us drink to the memory of those whom the Lord has taken unto Himself, and to those whose suffering continues on Armenian soil and to the soil which has been watered by so many tears. We have no other country. Whatever suffering she may have caused her people, we are her children.'

In the light of day Leninakan proved no less terrible a sight than by night. Now one could see things which the darkness had hidden: corpses laid out on the pavement in front of ruined houses, a dreadful cemetery amongst the living. Covered up any old how, these recently living people awaited their turn for the last hasty rites.

Hospital tents had been set up on the square in front of the district committee office of the Party right beside a statue of Lenin. Medical students were looking after two eighty-year-old women, Azni Mkrtychan and Tagun Berberyan. When the earthquake struck they had been sitting on a bench outside their home and in front of their very eyes their children and grandchildren had perished. Now young Muscovites were giving them bread and water, though they only wanted one thing – to be reunited with their children in the next life.

We went off to the polytechnic institute, where another sad sight awaited us: on the grass in front of the building were coffins draped in black crêpe and the textbooks of the young people who had died. Soldiers had formed a chain with the surviving students and were picking over the ruins stone by stone.

We wandered a bit further on to the area which the locals call the triangle, where nine-storey death-traps had been built. Only 5 or 6 out of 49 blocks were left standing, the rest had become nine-metre high tumuli. And on these burial mounds people were grubbing away, carefully trying to extricate the living or the dead. Soldiers with sappers shovels were picking at something in the rubble as there were not enough cranes. Someone from the army had a concrete block hooked on to a hawser attached to a tank. Some Armenians were trying to get hold of a girder with the pincers of a pipe-laying machine. But our impression was that the soldiers were no more organized than the civilians.

A reporter from one of the Siberian newspapers came up to me and told me that he had just been talking to an officer who had escorted a column of Armenian refugees from Azerbaijan. At the approaches to the frontier the convoy had been fired on and a soldier had been wounded. The escort had returned fire. There had also been losses on the attackers' side.

What a strange world this is. At the very time the Siberian was telling me about this Azerbaijani attack on Armenian refugees a military transport plane bringing aid to the Armenians in Leninakan had crashed. Among the dead were 50 Azerbaijanis. Apart from them, on the plane there were 13 Lezghins, 11 Russians, 2 Tartars, 1 Armenian and 1 Jew. They were all volunteers from a civil defence regiment, who had previously served in the army.

On 9 December the regiment was called up and was ready to fly from Baku, but take-off was delayed, according to the official announcement, because of bad weather. However, it in fact took off on the foggiest and most overcast day for ages. Some newspapers observed that well-wishers had pestered the passengers with such questions as 'Who asked you to stick your noses in down there?' and, 'Why are you flying off there of all places?' It is not impossible, therefore, that the two-day delay was not merely because of the bad weather.

The powerful Ilyushin-76 took off from Sumgait, carrying seventy rescue workers, two trucks and numerous tents, sleeping bags and rations. It had enough fuel to take it to Leninakan and back. On the landing approach one of the wings clipped the top of a mountain, and the plane crashed and broke up.

The sole survivor amongst the passengers and crew, a certain Fakhretdin Balaev, who, in defiance of instrutions, was lying alseep in the cab of a truck, was thrown clear of the aircraft when it crashed. Fully conscious, he ran away from the wreckage, fearing an explosion. It was later discovered that he had scrambled out and away with a fractured spine.

Afterwards, the commander in chief of the airforce, Marshal A. Efimov, commented on the tragic event: 'Flying is hazardous in Armenia. I myself served there in my time. The mountains create difficult meteorological conditions. In the opinion of Soviet aviation experts, we must consider the possibility of error by the pilot of the aircraft, airforce pilot first class Captain Nikolai Brilev. One of the possibilities is the following. The altitude meter would be set at the atmospheric pressure of the aerodrome. In the valleys, this is 760 mm, but the airport in Leninakan is situated at 1,500 metres above sea level and there the pressure would be 634 mm.

Even if, let us suppose, the commander set it at 734 mm, then the error in the altitude meter would be more than 1,000 metres. He could see the aerodrome and started his approach run. Under him and ahead there was total darkness. There was a mountain ahead, and the error in calculating his altitude then played its fatal role. . . .'

On the square a crowd had gathered, besieging the evacuation headquarters. On a side street was a long queue of mothers with children. Inside the building men were shouting. Worried militiamen were trying to calm people down.

Although a few hours beforehand Gorbachev had asked local men to stay behind to help with the rescue work, and send the women and children out first – and the crowd on the street had agreed with him – now a different picture was emerging. Sos Sarkisyan tried to dissuade the men, but they listened politely and continued their siege. We pushed our way outside again. Two lads were dragging a crate of Pepsi-Cola past the front of a wrecked church, only its chancel and facade were standing. This Pepsi-Cola was being given away free by a shop, and some were not merely taking what they needed but as much as they could carry away. Behind the lads with the crate was a little boy asking them to give him a bottle. The older boys were pretending not to hear him. The little boy ran over to us. Altogether he must have had ten bottles stuck in his pockets, down the front of his jacket and in his hands.

'Give us a drink,' said Armen.

The boy smiled but did not give him a bottle.

'It's not just the town that has been ruined, but the people.'

We went up to the church and sat on the stones which had once been a wall. Sos was weeping; he told Armen and me that he was thinking of an incident in his childhood. It is probably true, although I took it as a parable.

'When I was a boy,' said Sos, 'I lived on the outskirts of Stepanavan. There were only small houses and everyone knew everyone else. Not far from us there was a school, and the teacher there was a tall, red-haired man by the name of Ovanes. He was a quiet chap, who had never said a harsh word about anybody in

152

his life. But for some reason everyone felt that he knew all their misdeeds and bad thoughts about neighbours, although he was always pleasant and courteous. The women didn't even wear grubby pinafores around the house and, when he went down the street, the men didn't drink wine on weekdays, although he had never paid them a surprise visit in his life. Children studied, not from fear of being criticised by Ovanes, but from a desire to be praised by him. The houses on our street were cleaner than those on other streets and, when he went home from school, women used to stand at their gates waiting for him to walk by to say hello. If something bad had happened, they would ask Ovanes's advice, if something good, they would share their joy with him. When I was a teenager and wanted to become an actor, my mother said to me, "How happy Ovanes will be if you make people happy with your acting." She said Ovanes, not my father.

'Then one day he died. The men and women wept over his grave, remembering the good feelings which the red-haired teacher had evoked in them. But the morning after the funeral, I went out into the yard and overheard my mother saying to a neighbour that she was ashamed because she felt relieved somehow that Ovanes had died. And the neighbour said that she felt the same. And before long our street, relieved by the death of the red-haired man, was as dirty and messy as the others. The men started to drink again on weekdays and stopped shaving, and the women went for months without bothering to take off their dirty creased overalls, and the children studied for fear of being ticked off by their parents now that they were free of their former teacher's gaze....'

'Sos, Armen,' I said, 'you are going to put up a memorial to the victims of the earthquake. There is bound to be a competition. I have an idea. You see that half-destroyed church? Why don't you leave it just like that. Clean the mud and rubbish away. And inside, with subscriptions from everyone who wants to, build a smaller working chapel, like an offshoot from a plant.'

'Amen,' said Sos.

It was growing dark, time for us to leave. Sos raised his arm and the first car that had room for all three of us stopped. Within fifty metres it stopped again: ahead of us was an enormous traffic jam, cars were at a standstill four deep. I got out and walked ahead to see how long it would be before we were on the move again. It looked to me as though I had another couple of hours to walk around.

Along the pavement was a line of elderly women with prams loaded with suitcases and packages, many of them had children with them. They were all going in the same direction – out of town, in the hope that at the checkpoint the soldiers would put them into a car going to Erevan. These people had despaired of winning the battle for an organized evacuation. Those who had not been able to obtain a pram were carrying their belongings themselves.

On a street leading off the main road packed with cars a whole colony of young Russian women had sprung up. On the pavement stood salvaged tables and chairs at which, dressed in coats covered in blankets, these weavers, who had lived in the ruined hostel of a textile factory, had whiled away the four days since the earthquake. Right next to the roadway leading to the bridge, with its continuous rumble of trucks, they had set up folding beds made up with sheets upon which, under white coverlets, the girls slept in turns without getting undressed. Some of them were lying on mattresses right at the edge of the road. Their faces and hands were black with dust and four days' worth of dirt. There were neither toilets nor washing facilities anywhere near by.

The women had come here from various places to work on a temporary basis with the promise of possible earnings or the hope of making their lives in comfortable Leninakan. They had neither relatives nor close friends in the place. They were neither wounded nor dead, and therefore were condemned to be evacuated last of all from the scene of the disaster. Many of them had lost their few modest possessions, and some were without papers – they had lost their passports and their employment record books in which their previous places of work were recorded. These little books are more valuable to a Soviet worker than a passport: a lost passport can usually be quickly replaced, but a work book, upon which the level of one's future pension depends, is almost impossible to replace. Last of all they would receive, in the local district soviets, papers with a stamp confirming their identity, but only after the authorities were satisfied that the documents had genuinely been destroyed.

Right in the middle of the street a stove was burning just brightly enough to warm one's outstretched hands. Luckily there was an adequate supply of wooden debris from the ruins. There was a kettle on the stove. With a cup of hot tea inside you it is easier to keep going somehow. And it was possible to get water.

A mobile army water tanker stopped at the junction, and people immediately ran up with pots and pans or plastic canisters and formed a silent queue. An Austrian rescue team watched this queue impassively. They were neat and their camp was neat with its neat dogs, water, rations, pit props and motorcycles. They were like visitors from another planet. Further along, in the next house, some Englishmen were working alongside Soviet rescue workers; they looked more like people from our planet, covered in dust, tired and busy.

Here for the first time I saw some Soviet civil defence detachments in gas masks and protective overalls. They were clearing away corpses which had been lying in the rubble or in the streets for five days and nights already. God knows why I only ever saw one detachment properly dressed for the job like that. The rest whom I met in the earthquake disaster zone were loading corpses with their bare hands and without any special overalls or protective masks although the stench was already noticeable by the fourth day. Where had their equipment got to? Was it lying in some store? Perhaps it had been sent to Armenia, but they hadn't managed to distribute it?

'Why are the men collecting the bodies not dressed in protective clothing?' an Italian rescue worker asked me. 'I know we brought enough with us to Armenia to have seen them at least once.'

'What colour were they?'

The Italian understood what lay behind my question, he had already got the hang of Leninakan. 'No, they were black, like wetsuits. If they had been brightly coloured jumpsuits for the rescue workers like the Swedes sent, then it might have been possible that they thought it was a shame to get them dirty. But these ...'

'They'll have been put in store somewhere,' ventured a man from Minsk, who had joined the group for a smoke, 'then they'll come in handy for fishing. Let's go, Enzo.'

They were loading corpses on to a lorry, putting them first into coffins. A man was sitting on a crate nearby. He was making a list of the dead on a sheet of paper. 'Any documents on that one? No. OK. Let's put down male – that's for certain. Age. How old would you say he was, lads, by the look of him? Well, lets say forty. Next: girl aged seven. Now another man.'

In the past few days, the scribe had already scrutinised thousands of men, women and children of all ages, and was now totally unmoved. One could understand his reaction. It was either that or go out of your mind. Luckily the human mind is capable of protecting itself. However, nobody can get entirely used to death.

Various people helped the victims to bear their loss: relatives, friends, family and strangers who had come to the rescue. And faith helped. Faith, not in the traditional sense, habitual for peoples whose religious tendencies, although not in tune with the Soviet political system, nevertheless are the norm. Armenians are the oldest Christians on the territory of the Soviet Union. The roots of their culture and traditions, imbued with their national characteristics, are close to the culture of other Christians. But faith in a world beyond the grave, in spiritual salvation, as taught by the church, is to a great extent lost. The old churches lie empty, converted from places of worship into architectural testaments to their ancient historic culture. To a significant extent, also, the religious traditions observed by Christians in other countries have been lost. However, the authority of the Catholic Patriach of all Armenia, Vazgen I, is unusually great. In essence, he fulfils the role of father to this nation scattered throughout the world, uniting people through his unlimited authority – not only defender of the faith but also of the soul of the nation. Armenians trust him alone to intercede with God, to pray for them, to take upon himself their woes and rekindle their hopes.

Of course, it would probably have been easier to bear the

suffering and strengthen the soul if people had preserved their Christian faith and forms of worship, and if each person had been able himself or herself to pray for the safekeeping of their loved one in heaven. But only a few knew their prayers and held services, although many knew of the religious basis of the tragic history of their people.

While I was waiting for our car to get through the traffic jam, I wandered through the darkening streets of Leninakan. Thousands of Armenians were gathering in Echmiadzin for a service in memory of the victims of the earthquake, during which Vazgen I gave an address.

'According to the most recent figures, many tens of thousands of people have died. Thousands have been injured. Many thousands of families have been left without homes or shelter – they are wandering lost with shattered souls upon the mounds of rubble, seeking their dead, incapable of understanding what has happened to them, not in a state to wonder why such a disaster has befallen them. And even we here today are in a similar state of shock. So we can only pray for the peace and salvation of the souls of the dead.

'Beloved brothers and sisters, although we are all for obvious reasons feeling badly wounded and in despair, do not let us forget that we are Christians and throughout its history our believing people have many times had to suffer for various reasons martyrdom of a greater or lesser kind. Even the survival itself of the Armenian people seems like a miracle to modern historians. How did the Armenian people withstand and survive all their vicissitudes? How did they conquer the forces of death, how could they regenerate themselves?

'And today we are that same people and today also we do not wish to fear death, we do not wish to despair – and we must not. On the contrary, perhaps, after the first days of this tempest, we must make even greater efforts to preserve ourselves, our consciousness, all our spiritual forces, the unity of our people with our own national government – like one heart and one soul – to heal our wounds, ever casting our gaze towards heaven, there glimpsing the clear and burning stars of the hopes of our people.

Before and after death the unvanquished force of life springs eternal, giving birth ever anew to the flower of life.

'Beloved children, in this spirit and with this sacred faith, we offer up our prayer to God. And He will accept our prayers like incense, rising straight to the heights of heaven, and He will turn His face to us and will remain henceforth and for evermore our protector and guide, so that the Armenian people can continue their mission under the sun and reach new heights.

'Yea, we are strengthened by Thy precept, we gather our strength fearlessly and without complaint.

'The soul represents the unity of all man's creative powers, the synthesis whose secret our people possess and have proved it through the long centuries. Today also we are that same people who stand now unflinching before our fate, obeying Thy command – to live, to be and surmount all our difficulties.

'My dear sorrowing children, also in these tragic days we are deeply touched by all the sympathy and compassion, all the brotherly assistance which our people, our state and myself have received. First of all I would like to express my gratitude and praise to the whole Armenian people, both in Armenia and in the diaspora. I would also like to convey blessings to those young people, students, who in recent days, shoulder to shoulder with Soviet troops, have been voluntarily carrying out God's work, saving those still alive and bringing out the bodies of the dead from the ruins, helping the wounded and to some extent soothing the grief of all those who were suffering.

'I must also express my thanks to all our neighbouring brother peoples of the Soviet Union, to foreign governments and peoples, who stretched out the hand of assistance to our wounded Armenia so generously and so sincerely.

'I want to mention the telegram of sympathy from the Russian Orthodox Church and the donation by its head, the Holy Patriarch Pimen, of one million roubles; the words of sympathy from the Pope in Rome and his donation of 100,000 dollars; also the head of the Church of England, the Archbishop of Canterbury, whose efforts led to the donation by the British Government of a large sum to relieve the suffering of victims of the disaster. The cathedral church of Echmiadzin has placed 500,000 roubles from its slender means at the disposal of victims, which, taking into account the other donations already mentioned, brings the total to 1,700,000 roubles.

'This does not of course mean that our duty is done. I, as the head of the Armenian Church, as the first minister of the cathedral of Echmiadzin, will continue my efforts with the aim of collecting as many donations as possible. And may God grant that the rebuilding and rebirth of the devastated towns be greeted not by requiems for the dead, but by prayers of thanks.'

Hope activates man.

Along our familiar route, under the railway line just like the day before, the traffic jam gradually eased. A bus full of evacuated children moved, promising them a new life. A grim little boy, who had obviously lived through quite a bit these past few days, shyly smiled when he met me slung about with my camera equipment. His was the only smile I saw in all those days.

On our way out of town, we were stopped by a patrol. Armoured troop carriers and tanks blocked the road.

'Open your boot.'

We obeyed, knowing that this search was not just a formality. In recent days abandoned flats had been looted. Any good-for-nothing could break in under cover of darkness without the slightest risk of discovery and take what he wanted. The looting was concentrated on shops, where goods and valuables soon vanished from the ruins.

There is scum on the top of every broth. Armenia is no exception. Pillage is a word associated with war, but it is equally appropriate in the circumstances of the earthquake. In the past few days alone, soldiers and detachments of the Ministry of the Interior had arrested more than 150 people for taking goods, and more than 4,000,000 roubles in cash; more than 30,000 roubles alone were found in the possession of one lousy soldier called Bushlakov. There were attempts to loot bank safes in ruined buildings. Even television sets were taken from damaged stores

... So, being searched did not offend us.

'Have you caught many thieves?' I asked the sergeant.

'It has happened,' he replied meaningfully. 'So, would you like to see some? Then go and have a look at the heaps of rubble – there are plenty of "prospectors" there.'

The debris from the devastated buildings was not being taken far out of town, for drivers were saving time in order to make more trips. Heaps of rubble were growing all along the highway; it was only later that proper dumps were established for the debris. Thieves also came at night to forage in the remains. Using pocket torches, they picked over the debris and, so it was said, found cash and gold.

The highway to Erevan was guarded by troops at various points. We were not asked at the second or third checkpoints for documents nor were we searched – people were allowed away without hindrance – but those going into the area were being searched. Since the third day, private cars had been turned back from entering town unless they had a pass, but in Armenia, where everyone has many friends, obtaining a pass did not present a problem (even I had a pass issued for me by my friend Zori Balayan). For this reason the officers were interviewing everyone and deciding for themselves whom to allow into Leninakan and whom not to.

There was shouting, noise, people nearly came to blows. Some with a pass were not being allowed through – where was the justice in that? Of course, it was a disgrace. Such people were perhaps going to fetch their nearest and dearest (fair enough, but why so late in the day?) or to collect property belonging to their relations, but ... Thinking of the ambulances with their headlights blazing because every minute lost brought their passenger nearer to death, trying valiantly to get through the bottlenecks of cars, thinking of the evacuation bus so full of children that they were standing in the aisles, thinking of the cranes which could not get through to the places where they might save someone's life – in this situation I found myself on the side of the soldiers.

The whole way along the highway we met vehicles loaded with

equipment on their way to Leninakan.

When at last we entered Erevan and saw the high-rise blocks of the capital, Armen Oganesyan said, 'Please God these buildings won't be tested for their strength.' We were remembering the 'triangle' district in Leninakan.

In the hotel, which now resembled an international one because of the large numbers of foreigners who had come to assist, Zori Balayan was awaiting us.

'Gorbachev has held a conference,' he said. 'Ryzhkov has been given *carte blanche*. However, when Gorbachev left, he wasn't just upset by what he had seen but was also infuriated by what he had heard. From the crowds on the streets there were shouts about the Karabakh problem, about the children whom the authorities wanted to take out of Armenia. All the leaders of the movement whom the authorities managed to round up had been put in jail. This is not an appropriate time for arrests. You know that I disagreed with a lot of what they were doing, I didn't like it, but from an objective point of view even at the time of the clearing-up operation after the earthquake they were a great help, organizing people. Their influence on the people is considerable . . . I cannot forgive myself for having lost sight of them.'

We went up to the room where the thoughtful Balayan had arranged for a meal and a bottle of mulberry vodka.

'You must fly back to Moscow,' he said, 'the editor's waiting for your copy. Get it written and then come back. There are no air tickets to be had, the airport is snowed under, but I think we can fix something for you. I know the pilots.'

That night some of the journalists whom I had left waiting for Gorbachev at the airport came along to my room. It turned out that, because of the weather, they had spent a whole day waiting there. The press photographers who got to Leninakan had taken practically no pictures of Gorbachev, because Gorbachev had asked them as a personal favour not to, out of respect for the victims.

'He was shocked,' *Izvestiya* photographer Volodya Svartsevich told me, 'even stunned. I've seen him on many official visits. Usually he is quite in control of all his contacts with the public, he argues, appeals to his listeners, but this time he was not his usual self. He said very little, just nodded and listened. And Raisa Gorbachev also behaved differently from normal. In the crowd, people were asking why he brought her along.'

'He had no choice but to bring her. If she hadn't come, then it would have been said that, fine, she was happy enough to go to America with him but didn't so much fancy coming to the scene of the earthquake. So she came, and people then asked why.'

During the morning of 12 December I made my way over to Trade Unions House. Somebody had told me the day before that the money they were supposed to be paying out to the victims was not being distributed because of the crush.

It was impossible to drive up to Trade Unions House because soldiers were keeping cars away, but it only took me five minutes to walk there. At the door of the building there was a small crowd, which looked like the end of a queue. In the empty hall there were tables at which victims were asked to sit. They showed their passport or their substitute document certifying how many dependents they had and handed their document over. Clerks took down their details and wrote a chit to the cashier, who took the cash out of a Salamander shoe box, stamped their passport or whatever and gave them 100 roubles for every surviving person. This was trade union assistance to workers in the textile industry.

'Any problems?' I asked the cashier.

'No. Sometimes there are misunderstandings – people trying to get something they're not entitled to – but otherwise everything's going fine.'

In the hour or so that I spent there, there was only one attempt to swindle the system. A young woman showed her passport and explained something in Armenian. When she had been given a chit, she went up to the cashier. They talked briefly, after which she went out without obtaining any money.

'What happened?'

'A lot of people who worked in the factory in Leninakan were registered in Erevan. That's why it's difficult to check whether or not they're genuine victims. We have to take their word for it, but we do ask at least which workshop they were in, who they knew there, who the director was, just to check. That woman didn't even know whereabouts in town the factory was. That means she was trying to cheat the system.'

It was obviously difficult to single out the genuine victims, and how could the state compensate them for the losses they had suffered? In the earthquake zone there were more than 700,000 people – some had lost everything, some nothing.

'There are no laws on the subject,' said Davyatin, a lawyer from the Ministry of Finance. 'Commissions made up of representatives of the trade unions, Department of Social Security, financial institutions and industrial firms will decide the size of compensation.'

'But if someone has lost everything, how will it be decided what the loss was?'

'Basically according to evidence brought by the victim, witnesses, any documents they have salvaged.'

'But how much will each victim receive regardless of the extent of his material loss?'

'A one-off payment of 200 roubles. Families who've lost their breadwinner will receive 2,000 roubles in addition. Above that they'll receive 500 roubles to pay for the funeral of each dead member of the family. That's all the state is providing. On top of that, victims will be obtaining money from their trade union, social funds, private individuals, etc. There are quite a few complications here – many people have left the area, but the registration points are all situated in Erevan. It's easier for those who can obtain their money here, but those who've left the republic have to write to the executive committee. And they have to reply.'

'It sounds complicated. And how about compensation for lost property?'

'Anyone who had insurance will get the insurance for their lost property, but insurance isn't very common round here. The State has decided to pay everyone compensation for their home, their garage, their car, their own pig, cow or whatever, based on realistic valuation. Apart from that, for their furniture and household effects single people are to receive 4,000 roubles (the equivalent of eighteen months' average salary). A family of two will receive 7,000 plus 500 for every further member of the family. For instance, a family of six will receive 13,000. All loans taken out by citizens, let's say for building work, will be taken over and paid for out of the republic's budget.'

'And what's to be done with orphans, the wounded and disabled?'

'They'll all receive a pension regardless of age and work status. Children will receive a maximum pension dating from the day of their parents' death. Adults depending on their salary from their last place of work.'

'Thousands of women and children were evacuated to various towns and are living on state security, but they still need money, nevertheless.'

'Mothers with children not yet of age who've lost their jobs are being paid their average wage until they manage to find a new one, but only for six months. Those who've gone away to rest homes and sanatoria will also be on half pay for six months.'

The modest sums mentioned in these answers give a general idea of the financial difficulties with which the victims would be contending, despite the help they were entitled to receive. We know all too well the diminishing effect which such an experience produces. To begin with there is a powerful wave of genuine sympathy, then, as the affair loses its emotional appeal, there is a diminution of interest, it becomes routine, boring. It was the same with Chernobyl. When it had just happened – all zeal, all passionate propaganda efforts, vehicles, people and state assistance poured in. A peak is reached, when public goodwill is aroused to the maximum. Then, one day, all the big shots from the Government and the newspapermen leave, and people are left alone with their misfortune.

When I got back to my room, I found Zori waiting for me. He looked like thunder.

'While we were away in Leninakan, terrible things have been happening here. The day after the arrests, yesterday, the troops clashed with demonstrators. What a disaster!'

Just what a disaster it had been I found out later, when I was told the details of the previous day's events which had taken place with the participation of members of the Karabakh Committee. They had worked from the very first minute that they had heard about the earthquake. They had set up their headquarters in the Writers' Union and had prided themselves as helpers of the Government commission. In the prevailing conditions of panic and confusion, they took on the function of coordinators, which they turned their hands to quite well. They had set up offices in Spitak and Leninakan. They sent their activists to the accessible country districts. The Committee formed teams with equipment and sent between sixty and seventy manned buses to the earthquake disaster area. They also evacuated people and arranged for them to be put up with families. They had been recording the names of thousands of people who wished to take in victims and foster orphans. Rumours continued to circulate in Erevan and members of the Committee, using their authority, took upon themselves to emphasise to people the absurdity of suggestions that the earthquake was an artificially created event and the absurdity of the fantasy about children being taken away from Armenia for good. They also established control over the arriving aid. And made contact with the French singer Charles Aznavour and the Governor of California, John Tokmedzhan (both Armenians by origin), asking them to organize the European and American relief funds and take complete control of their distribution. These funds were to be handed over directly to Armenians, by-passing state distribution channels – a move unlikely to be welcomed by the authorities.

On 10 December, several hundred women who wanted to adopt orphans gathered at the Writers Union, where the Karabakh Committee was based. They were desperately worried by rumours that people outside Armenia were volunteering to take children.

Ashot Manucharyan, with the approval of the District Military Commandant, made a speech to the women gathered there, saying, 'We are very grateful for your kind offers, but we are proposing to keep all the orphans in Armenia in a special nursery. The question of adoption is going to be settled after the rescue work is over.'

The women dispersed, reassured. But within two hours more arrived. The District Commander ordered them to return to their homes. Manucharyan begged them to do so since people were awaiting the arrival in half an hour of buses from the earthquake zone.

After half an hour, the District Commander came back with the new City Commandant, General Mokashev, with another request to the crowd to disperse immediately. The members of the Committee refused, because they were responsible for the organization of rescue work and were not holding a meeting.

'Brother officers, are you ready to do your duty?'

'We are.'

They arrested Ashot Manucharyan, Khachik Stamboltsyan (both deputies of the Supreme Soviet of the Armenian Soviet Socialist Republic), Babken Araktsiyan, Vazgen Manukyan and Samvel Gevorkyan.

Alekan Akopyan was in a nextdoor room sorting clothes and came into the office at the moment when the five of them were being led off under guard. 'What's going on? Are you arresting the Karabakh Committee?' he asked.

'Yes. What's that to you?'

'I'm a member of it as well.'

'You'd better come along with us then.'

Ambartsum Galstyan, who had been busy elsewhere, came in just as they were being taken away with an escort of machine-guns, colonels and a general.

'What's going on?' he asked Vazgen Manukyan in Armenian.

'Go away, don't get mixed up in this,' replied Vazgen.

Galstyan thought they were being taken in under some minor powers of detention: Why should I go and sit in jail with them for three days? Let them go and have a bit of a rest, and I'll get on with the work, he thought to himself.

Ashot Manucharyan asked the military authorities to show him the decision of the Praesidium of the Supreme Soviet enabling them thus to violate his rights as a deputy. They assured him that he had not been arrested, merely detained. As soon as they established his rights as a deputy, he was released.

'Up to that moment', Manucharyan later wrote in hiding, 'we had worked completely constructively with the existing directorate of the town, avoiding any difficulties arising out of various incidents. We had called on the people to behave with restraint and, if there were complaints about the actions of the troops, we submitted them to the Commandant's office and sorted it out with him in a businesslike way. Everything we did made it possible for us all to get through a difficult situation without serious incident. I calculated that it was still possible to save the situation by appealing on television to the population to keep calm and say that what had happened was a mistake, if all those who had been arrested at the Writers Union were released. I received assurances on this point and, having reached agreement, I thanked them warmly and left, confident that the incident was closed.'

The following day, on 11 December, he was told that those who had been 'detained' were not 'under arrest'. People rang him up to find out the details, so he decided to meet them to explain the circumstances of the arrests.

About a thousand people surrounded by troops were waiting for him beside the statue to Tamanyan. Manucharyan decided to lead them through the centre of the city to publicize what had happened. By the Rossiya film theatre their way was blocked by tanks, so the crowd turned towards the Gayane film theatre, where the Deputy City Commandant announced that the Moscow Procurator's office was in charge of the detained members of the Committee and warned that, if the crowd did not disperse, they would be driven forcibly away. The crowd did not disperse, the march continued. At the railway bridge soldiers attacked the crowd. People ran away towards the square and started throwing stones at the troops. A battle began.

The Soviet Union as a whole heard about these events from an interview with Gorbachev, and by the same token the newspapers began to accuse the Karabakh Committee of many crimes, to which Manucharyan replied: 'It is a lie that the activists in the movement did not take part in the rescue work in the earthquake zone. The overwhelming majority of the activists were in the disaster area, not one of them will leave his post until the rescue work is finished. It is a lie that the movement organized any sort of meetings after 7 December. It is a lie that the committee participated in any way in spreading panic rumours.'

Fear gave these rumours momentum, and the Committee issued corrections and calmed people down (as far as it could.) It was a lie that the Committee was longing for power – it had been decided internally that any member of the Committee who accepted an official post automatically lost the moral right to belong to the Committee. It was also a lie that the Committee was against the sending of victims for recuperation to sanatoria and rest homes in the Soviet Union.

After the events of 11 December the Committee members, Ambartsum Galstyan, Ashot Manucharyan, Vano Siradetyan, Samson Kazaryan, David Vardanyan and Rafael Kazaryan, went underground. However, Kazaryan, who could not take living illegally, presented himself at the commandatura and signed an undertaking not to leave the city.

On 12 December my newspaper rang me and told me to fly straight back to Moscow to write an article for the next issue.

I consulted with Zori about what to say in the piece and we went together to Zvartnots airport, which was overflowing with incoming aircraft. That very day Gorbachev was flying out of Armenia, which put an additional nervous strain on the air traffic controllers, who were already at their wits' end. They allowed incoming foreign aircraft to land out of turn. Language difficulties complicated the situation to the limits.

All the parking bays were occupied by enormous aircraft and some were also parked on the taxiways. Despite having brought in hundreds of the cranes and lorries by air, nobody thought of obtaining even a couple of additional airport tractors. It was sheer luck that there were only three air crashes altogether.

I had no plane ticket, but this did not seem to worry Balayan, who drove straight on to the runway, where an airbus Ilyushin-86 was standing with its engines turning. Apparently not a single passenger aircraft had flown out to Moscow that day and this airbus getting ready for takeoff had been full of passengers since morning.

The captain of the aircraft, Dmitri Adbashyan, seemed to be a friend of Balayan's. He sat me in the cabin and we continued to wait for permission to take off. Ahead of us on the runway was some sort of Middle Eastern airliner. Beyond that a Soviet Ilyushin-76 was blocking the way; taxi-ing out it had tipped an American Boeing with its wing. Nobody from the airport staff was with any of the airplanes; it took two hours to clear the runway. The passengers in our cabin began to mutiny, asking to be let out as they were afraid there might be something mechanically wrong with our aircraft. At the same time, the wireless in the cabin was switched on and all the conversations between arriving aircraft and the control tower were clearly audible. They were the usual laconic and traditional exchanges. Suddenly we heard a voice with a foreign accent pleading, 'We are on our approach run to the airport, please be good enough to give us a position and altitude - please.'

'How polite,' said one of our officers. 'They should ask a bit louder and more rudely. It must be a plane from the Baltic states or somewhere.'

'Please, we are a Yugoslavian aircraft. Please advise us of our landing instructions.'

The following day we learned that we were probably the last people to hear the Yugoslavian crew. Their Antonov-12 crashed on its landing approach somewhere in the area of the Echmiadzin highway.

In Moscow I postponed my piece until the following week's issue so that I would have time to write it up properly, and one evening I went to visit the eminent physicist Andrei Sakharov, who was taking a great interest in the earthquake. It turned out that he wanted very much to pay a visit to Armenia, Azerbaijan and

Karabakh, but did not know how to organize it because of the state of emergency. It seemed to me there would be no difficulty arranging such a trip if he approached Alexander Yakovlev, with whom he had had meetings.

Later I was told that Sakharov received an appointment to meet Yakovlev immediately. During their conversation, Yakovlev rang Gorbachev, who supported the idea: 'Let them go, have a look and assess the real situation.' I felt that neither the Central Committee in Moscow nor Sakharov had sufficient objective information. Any of his subsequent speeches on the subject of the problems which had arisen in Armenia, Azerbaijan and Nagorny Karabakh would have been open to charges of prejudice based on hearsay if he had not made this journey.

The group consisted of Andrei Sakharov and his wife Yelena Bonner, the ethnopsychologist Galina Starovoitova and historians Leonid Batkin and Andrei Zubov.

In Baku they had a meeting with Vezirov, the first secretary of the Central Committee of the Communist party of Azerbaijan, and various members of the scientific and artistic intelligentsia. The authority of Sakharov is high in such circles in the Soviet Union, but on this occasion the writers and scientists of the republic did not treat him very respectfully. They talked among themselves during his speech calling for a reasoned resolution to the conflict, openly turning their backs on him and rattling their keys. Nevertheless, Sakharov told me that his visit to Baku was extremely useful. He realized that it would not be possible to ignore the arguments of the Azerbaijanis; the movement which had sprung up there deserved study and could not merely be dismissed as extreme radicalism and intolerance. It shamed him that, with very few exceptions, even the left wing of the intelligentsia did not condemn the butchery at Sumgait. Many of the Baku intelligentsia considered that the Armenians had an innate ethnic and historic need to suffer and thereby to seek worldwide sympathy. Therefore, according to them, Sumgait was provoked by Armenians as a result of a perceived shortage of sympathy!

I flew from Moscow to Erevan for the second time since the earthquake to catch up with Sakharov's group in Nagorny Karabakh, in Stepanakert. The situation there was tense. Upon arrival at the airfield it was immediately apparent that the military were everywhere. The document checkpoint at the foot of the aircraft steps was guarded by soldiers with machine-guns, and armoured personnel carriers were positioned by the radar scanners next to the runway. There were guards at all the gates and doors. An officer had been warned of my arrival and, because of that, I was ushered straight through the building out to where a few private taxis were waiting for customers.

The road into town lies between tree-covered mountains. In several places it was punctuated by army control points with light tanks, but we were not stopped for document checks. Thus we made our way into the centre of town. The district Party committee building had soldiers in flak jackets stationed outside it. They were quite courteous and in answer to my question about what the news was in town, one of them told me people had gathered at the executive committee building awaiting Sakharov's visit only to be told that the meeting would be in the evening and so they had dispersed.

Within a few minutes Sakharov came out of the building with my friends Zori Balayan, Genrikh Pogosyan, the secretary of the district committee of the Party, and Arkady Volsky. Together we set off for the town of Shusha, which, in contrast to Stepanakert, was controlled by the Azerbaijanis.

A strange atmosphere had developed in Nagorny Karabakh. The sun was shining, the surroundings were beautiful, everything seemed peaceful, but the whole time it felt as though a war was going on. This microscopic state was guarding its borders fiercely. Armenian children and adults would not even go into the woods if they bordered on an Azerbaijani area, and *vice versa*. A barrier across the road backed up with machine-guns bore witness that we had left the Armenian sector of Karabakh and had entered the Azerbaijani one.

Our cars were by this time approaching Shusha, an ancient town in which many of the leading intellectuals of both republics had been born and the third largest in the Caucasus. At the beginning of the century the population was almost equally divided between Armenians and Azerbaijanis. Since then it had been more or less halved in number and of the 20,000 who remained, only thirteen per cent were Armenians. But now there were none – they had all fled, leaving their homes, which had suffered attacks basically from Azerbaijani refugees from Armenia.

There were two meetings arranged for the day, one in Shusha and another in Stepanakert, at which both sides asserted they were in the right. There was an interesting incident connected with the Armenian and Azerbaijani conflict at the Children's Hospital. Three little boys of the same nationality tortured a fourth of another nationality in their ward with naked high-voltage electric wires. He jumped out of a window, unable to bear the torture.

'I am deliberately not going to reveal which of the boys was Armenian and which Azerbaijani, and I don't know which of them to pity more,' said Bonner, 'the one who suffered physically or the three whose souls had been damaged. After the meetings I asked some of those who had attended it which nationality, in their opinion, was the boy who had jumped out of the window. In Shusha they said Azerbaijani, in Stepanakert they said Armenian.'

None of the refugees wished to return home. Even in Stepanakert where there were fifty to a class in the schools, lice in the kindergartens, and two babies to every cot in the hospital. In many places there was no television, and it was difficult to find work and drinking water.

The next morning we caught a flight to Leninakan, having spent the night at Stepanakert. The weather, however, forced us to land in Erevan and there representatives of Zori's inexhaustible supply of friends collected us, and transferred us to a helicopter, which flew to the devastated village of Luisakhbor already described. Erevan airport was more or less back to normal. Just over two weeks had gone by since the earthquake and it was as if, with the departure of Ryzhkov, the President of the Council of Ministers, who was heading the commission, the white-hot level of interest had begun to cool. Out of fifty-eight totally destroyed villages, nine had still received no help as yet.

Baskets and crates were being loaded into the helicopter; the loaders knew roughly what was in the crates. None of them had been in the village we were setting off to, knew how many people were left there nor what they needed. Just in case, they added a carton of baby food to the oats and tinned meat. Clothing had also been thrown in at random.

We got into the helicopter. Apparently Sakharov had never flown in one. During the years that he was working on the hydrogen bomb, he had had a plane at his disposal. The era of the helicopter came later.

In the few days that I had been out of Armenia, the landscape had changed – snow had fallen. In the earthquake zone the temperature dropped as low as $-10°C$. Flying below the mountain peaks, we landed in the village of Luisakhbor. People ran out from the nearby houses through the snow – men and women with children. Some young men had a very purposeful look about them.

Unloading began. The healthiest and most active came right into the helicopter and passed out the baskets and crates. Suddenly one young man seized a basket and went to the road, where a car was parked. An old woman took charge of a second basket and dragged it to the village, whence her daughter came to help her in a hurry. Another old woman, snatching a bundle of clothes, began to hobble away. She opened it a little way away at one side, saw that there were only children's things in it, threw it down on the snow, and came back to the helicopter. Zori watched all this with tears in his eyes, then he shook himself, got hold of a young man, brought him to the helicopter and started to organize the proper distribution of food. They loaded everything on a transport trailer, but, as soon as they got it moving, people started to pull off baskets and hampers and drag what had been brought for everyone away to their own houses. The effect of the earthquake was continuing – it was going on in the souls of these unfortunates who had lost their faith in people.

'What have we done to them?' wailed Balayan. 'Can you imagine a scene like this in a village before the earthquake?'

Next to Sakharov stood a man who was not taking part in the

distribution of aid. He had lost his wife and two daughters, and he did not need anything. From the jostling crowd a woman came up whose husband had died, but she had been left with eight children on her hands. She pleaded with the aircrew and the men by the remaining open boxes, but, apart from the parcel of children's things which the old woman had thrown aside, she got nothing.

Why was it necessary to humiliate people like that, tossing food and other goods into the crowd? The strong, who were possibly not in need, received, whereas the weak did not even get as far as the helicopter. Our country has a whole class of bureaucrats, but not even a hundred could be found to land in villages to organize fair distribution of the aid which had come from all over the world. Perhaps there were places where it was properly organized, but I never saw them.

Later, I parted company with the Sakharov group and went to the village of Dzhrashen to look at some medical stations which had been established in Central Asian *yurtas* (traditional circular nomad tents). The village was quite near the road and there was no difficulty in getting food to it, but in the square the people standing there were unshaven and strained-looking.

'Listen, we have had to hang about here all day. This morning we queued for food coupons. [By now a rationing system had been introduced in the earthquake zones.] Then again this evening for the food itself. If they bring it. At least they've given us the little bits of paper.'

They started to show me the coupons, of which there were quite a few, and to grumble at the chairman of the village soviet. The chairman – a nice man – explained that everything which had been brought would be distributed, but there was not enough of it.

'And where are the goods from abroad that I heard about on the radio?' asked a particularly active campaigner for truth.

'What the hell has that got to do with it?' asked the chairman. 'I've given you two new pairs of boots, but you're still going about in your old, worn out ones.'

Outside the shop where they were waiting for food there were traces of a campfire.

'We're peasants, we can't wait around all day for them to deign to serve us, we have work to do – mend the houses and get ready for spring. It's impossible for Ryzhkov to take control of the distribution of food and other things. We're grateful to him for his concern and effort. He demonstrates his sympathy when he talks to people, he takes his hat off when he talks to us because he understands that everyone may have lost a member of the family in the disaster. But big Armenian bureaucrats are going round the country with him, they are escorting him – so who's doing their work for them at the moment?'

Behind the words of this unshaven man in his cap lay a question which cropped up fairly often in Armenia at that time. Prime Minister Ryzhkov had won great popularity because of his genuine interest in people's plight. Faced with an acute situation, with problems for once not to do with state policy, hidden from the public gaze and befogged by commentators but with the problems of real people, he demonstrated humanity, and this was much appreciated. When it came to it, he was on the side of the ordinary Soviet citizen contending with the bureaucratic machine, the inertia and red tape of the ministries, he was on our side of the barricades. I think this is what explains his public reproof to various respected departments of state for their lamentable performance. They had not been up to much before, but Ryzhkov had seen it from the other side and had not noticed, or he had noticed but had said nothing, or he had spoken out unbeknownst to us, behind the scenes. But now he declared openly to the whole of the Soviet Union that it was a disgrace that not even interpreters had been provided for the foreign doctors who had flown in to help, that it was not even known how they were managing or what they needed. After this a representative of the powerful Ministry of Foreign Affairs babbled something indistinct, and within a day the Deputy Minister was in Erevan sorting things out.

On the other hand, if the truth be told, Ryzhkov's visits to the scenes of disaster also made the rescue and clearing work more difficult because, for security reasons, they closed the roads for him.

The usual efforts of functionaries to show themselves in the best possible light and throw dust in the eyes of the top leadership were made even in these sorrowful days. Some mountain climbers told me one typical example of this.

A grain elevator which was leaning like the tower of Pisa should have been demolished long before, but the officer in charge decided to wait for the Prime Minister's visit. He hired some civilian climbing enthusiasts, got them to secure one end of a cable to the elevator's top floor window-frames and the other end to a tank. Then they waited. Ryzhkov duly arrived with some television reporters prepared to film the sensational collapse. However, the tower stood firm and the window frames simply flew out. Ryzhkov went on his way. The army fastened the cables again and settled down to wait for Ryzhkov to return once more. But a second time they failed to demonstrate the army's magnificent efficiency, the tower still stood. This time Ryzhkov told them to stop mucking around, and the following morning they blew it up.

All this happened in Spitak not long before I flew there for a second time, with Sakharov's party.

It was a different place – deserted and cold, and the helicopter did not land in the stadium this time. There were no more coffins in the streets, they were stacked in the cemetery. There was much less traffic and no more jams at the crossroads. But here and there people were still picking through the rubble. Tents had sprung up around the stadium and on the pitch there was a long, white mobile hospital, a gift from the Norwegians. It was not yet in commission, unlike the hospital in Kirovakan, where Israeli doctors had long and successfully been at work, carrying out complicated operations and teaching the local doctors how to use equipment unfamiliar to them.

Having circled over Spitak, the helicopter found a landing pad the other side of the river, quite a long way from the centre.

The sight of the devastated town profoundly depressed my travelling companions, as they wandered among the ruins in a state of shock. Next to the landing pad there was a school: there were text books, exercise books, satchels ... the ruins of a kindergarten with broken toys. It was here that Sakharov said the devastation was similar to that which would be produced by a one-megaton atom bomb.

Some people emerged from the ruins.

'There's not much going on here.'

'Most people have left town,' said Sasha Tokarev, a student from Moscow. 'The big push is over. We've done what we can. There are no more survivors under the rubble. Ryzhkov has gone back to Moscow. Everything's quietened down.'

'Will you have cleared the rubble by Spring?'

The group of building workers shook their heads. 'You see, there are either people but no equipment or equipment but no people. Just like always – there are no good organizers. Its every man for himself, foraging for tools and deciding where to work. And they don't bring us any food or clothing.'

Across the river in the centre things were busier. There, a distribution exchange had been set up, and at the exchange people were pushing and shoving as if it were a market square. The Commandant of the first area of Spitak, Lieutenant Colonel Valery Gogunov, in answer to my question as to why there were not enough stoves, took me by the arm and led me to a big army tent where two stoves had been set up inside and four spares were lying about nearby. Gogunov's eyes were bloodshot and a star on one of his epaulettes was missing.

'We don't know these people, we don't know their language. How can we find out what they need? Where are the local officials, what are they doing about it? Here each person has a *yurta* and a tent. They sleep in a tent with a stove. But in area three, three hundred metres away, people are having to make their own shelters from the debris.'

We were standing right near these shanty-dwellers.

'They left a tank here to guard the road. It was here for four days without soldiers. It was in the way. The people themselves managed somehow to move it. Then the soldiers came back and moved it back to where it was.'

In the centre of the area a troop of soldiers in gas masks was salvaging rolls of wallpaper from the rubble of a furniture shop. They said, 'Our real job is to look for corpses, but while there are none of those we decided to pick over this place. As soon as we've found all the bodies, we'll flatten all the rubble and clear it away with bulldozers.'

'Will you clear away all the debris by Spring?'

The captain looked at the official party of strangers who had just arrived in their own helicopter and replied boldly, 'Yes, absolutely.'

'Up until which day were you still finding people alive?'

'We dug out a little girl on the eighth day. We thought she was dead. When the shovel touched her, she groaned. But whether or not she lived, we don't know'.

A lone man was digging in the rubble under the walls of his collapsed house. Nover Pogosyan was looking for his passport. He had found his wife and two children already, and now they were lying together in the cemetery on the hill.

'We're on our own now. For the first few days there was concern and help. Now they've salved their consciences and gone away. We're grateful. Everyone's got to get on with his own life. I am going to leave too, only first I must find my passport.'

A boy in an army balaclava who said his name was Ararat Nazaretyan was not even looking for his passport. His mother and sister had died, his brother had had one leg amputated, his father was in hospital, so he had built himself a little shack out of plywood and was living there, helping his neighbours.

'It's going to be cold in winter. How are you going to manage?'

'I'll survive. I'm going to wait for my father, otherwise we'll not find each other. I don't know which town they took him to.'

Ararat looked at me inquiringly. I told him that there was an information service which would help him find his father, but the boy did not believe me.

My companions were getting ready to take off again – the weather was closing in. I promised to rendezvous with them in Erevan and went off to Spitak stadium.

On the white snow was the enormous tent of the Norwegian

field hospital, and beyond it the little tented town of the counter-epidemic service. In Moscow from time to time there were frightening rumours about the possibility of epidemics following the earthquake. The situation was certainly very dangerous: as a result of the movement of the ground, water from the sewers had mixed with the drinking supply. The mains had had to be turned off, and all the wells in the neighbourhood were sealed. Water was being brought in by tanker from neighbouring regions, but the situation remained extremely difficult. A large number of mice had appeared, especially in the area of the grain elevator, where grain had spilled from broken containers. Rodents are potential spreaders of disease and they had to be destroyed. Hundreds of thousands of head of cattle lay dead under the ruins; they would have to be re-buried. The counter-epidemic service warned of possible outbreaks. Microbiologists from Moscow were working to the point of exhaustion. In the tents, the water froze by morning. There was no hot food and they were cultivating vital bacteria in thermos flasks.

'How do you see the problems?' I asked the head of the USSR sanitary service, Doctor V. Kartusev.

'There's no threat of an epidemic, at least until the Spring. There is some danger from stray dogs, there may be cases of rabies. It's difficult to arrange for individual livestock to be buried. There are no bathing or washing facilities as yet, so there is therefore a danger of lice and typhoid fever. But I think that we are on top of those problems. They are seeing to the relaying of water pipelines now. But it isn't only the water supply that's being seen to,' he smiled sadly. 'Someone has also seen to the generator from the water purification plant – a great big generator has been stolen, we can't find it anywhere.'

'What do you think, as a doctor, of the suggestion that Spitak should be rebuilt elsewhere?'

'I suppose it really ought to be.'

I had reconnoitred for my night's lodging and found a place with some climbing enthusiasts from Moscow. Their tent was small and cold, but in a warm sleeping bag it was perfectly comfortable. My host, Oleg Pankratev, kept me entertained until morning with reminiscences and musings about life in Spitak. He began by making the point that the Soviet Union does not have a single special service for major natural disasters.

'But surely there is – what about the civil defence force?' I asked, knowing the answer in advance.

'Well, they turned up on the 20th of December,' Oleg pulled a face. 'We were working on a site, then they came along, about twenty blokes dressed in black and tried to work alongside us, but we finally had to ask them to go away for fear that they were going to kill either themselves or us by mistake. They didn't even know which direction to tackle a ruined house from.'

'And have you worked alongside any of the rescue workers from abroad?'

'Yes, with the French, Italians, English and Poles. The Italians were the first to arrive and were falling over themselves. They hardly did any digging, but used their sniffer dogs and probes. Their dogs and the French and Polish dogs were from the fire service, trained to work in houses, but they only knew how to look for live people. If a dog found a body, it would cower and whine as if it was responsible for the person's death. After that, the dog had to be patted and encouraged. There were various sorts of dog. Mostly alsatians, but there were also terriers and retrievers. They were all very friendly and good natured. But some of the dogs felt uncomfortable because they were used to working at finding people in the snow.'

'Did you ask the foreign rescue workers how they thought the sort of destruction they found when they got to Armenia differed from the Mexican earthquake?'

'The French said that in Mexico, when the buildings collapsed, they made cavities. The beams held up against each other. Here that only happened in workshops where the ceiling fell on machine tools, but all the residential buildings collapsed into dust. Even if a man was not injured, he would be suffocated by breathing in earth he was buried in.

'Who did you like working with best?'

'It was pretty good working with everyone, but some of them had their own particular routines as far as eating and sleeping were concerned. Some did a bit of work that was their particular speciality, let us say, while others stood back a bit standoffishly. There was one occasion when I had to ask for some help from the English. I made radio contact and was told that the Brits were working on some ruins just round the corner. We went round there and found some men digging away, dressed in green ordinary looking gear. It never crossed my mind that it could be anyone other than Soviets. We looked everywhere and couldn't find anyone. It turned out that the chaps in green were Englishmen. They were working quietly away not asking anyone anything, not only using probes but also their bare hands. And they worked without breaks or resting.'

I watched various rescue teams at work and have the highest praise for their professionalism and care.

In Leninakan, where I went the following morning, things were busier than in Spitak. There was traffic on the roads and people were standing in queues for food rations.

The rations were given out in exchange for coupons and were unexpectedly meagre: 200 grams of sausage, a little packet of butter, a bit of cheese and bread. Of course, nobody was going to die of starvation. . . . The demographic make-up of the town had changed greatly; the majority of women and children had left. Some of the men had stayed behind to work, although far from all of them were fit. Thus, Leninakan was now mainly inhabited by families whose homes (basically, private ones) had remained intact, whose belongings were still there and who had provisions, although people had suffered among these families. The children were at school, the adults were at work, and the only people on the streets were engineers, soldiers and rescue workers on their way to work.

The goods which had been sent to help were especially needed in the first days when people were practically naked on the streets and any sort of clothing was gratefully received. Now, dressed in any old things, they had been dispersed throughout the country and there was nobody left in Leninakan who needed a new sweater or a child's overcoat. But these things continued to be sent with the best of intentions and were distributed, although they were no longer needed. At the Red Cross post they were handing out children's parcels with toys and clothes. Even people who had no children (in all, there were only 5,000 under the age of eighteen left in the town) took these parcels, undid them in the yard and left them there, taking only the things which were of any use to them. To me this meant that the aid had achieved its aim: when there is real need, you take without picking and choosing.

'Yes, the situation in Leninakan is already stable.' I was on my way with the Leninakan Health Services director Lavrenty Sudzhyan to look at a hospital which had been prepared to receive patients, although there were only a few of them.

'How many patients did you have in the first few days?'

'On the 7th of December 4,540, on the 8th 625, on the 9th 198, and after the 9th of December, when 150 were brought in, there was a sharp fall off in numbers.'

'When was the last person rescued alive in Leninakan?'

'The last reliably known to me was on the eighteenth day, but I don't know whether he survived.'

After that the newspapers printed two sensational reports. The first claimed that in Spitak in the ruins of an elevator they dug out eighteen people who had spent more than twenty-five days under the rubble. Anyone who had been in Spitak knew that this was impossible, but the report was widely reprinted. It had become boring to write about mundane essentials. People wanted a miracle; there were no miracles. The report turned out to be a lie.

A short while later, there was a second news story which was even more fantastic and caught the readers' imaginaton. TASS correspondents reported a sensation to the whole world: on the thirty-fifth day after the earthquake, in Leninakan, under the ruins of Bu Street six men had been rescued alive. One of them, a fifty-year-old electrician named Aykhaz Akopyan was brought by his own sister to clinical hospital number 3 in Erevan. The other five had apparently walked away, nobody knew where. According to the report, Akopyan and his colleagues Simonyan, Khachatryan, Sarkisyan and two others whose names Akopyan could not remember even after spending thirty-five days with them were preparing to move two enormous vats when suddenly the earthquake struck and all six found themselves trapped in the ruins. Sarkisyan suffered a broken arm, the others only had cuts and grazes. In the cellar there were homemade jams and smoked ham. The buried men lost count of time, but believed that they would be rescued. How and when they were rescued, Akopyan did not say.

An interview with the rescued electrician was broadcast on television. He looked a humble man and talked with difficulty. It would have been cruel to charge him with deception, all the more so since a psychiatrist told reporters who came to visit Akopyan that he was suffering from nervous exhaustion. He was still afraid of falling rubble and asked for his head to be protected. Nevertheless, he remembered what it was like in the cellar and talked about his family, apparently unaware that his wife and children had died.

'It looks as though he is telling the truth,' concluded the doctor.

I rang the Ministry, suspecting that the whole thing had been invented. I wanted to know why. I spoke to my friend Armen Atobikyan, a section manager, and established that this man's five companions had not been traced. Nor had they been found in any hospital in Armenia. The story now aroused his suspicions, although Akopyan was ill – he had heart disease. Armen excluded the possibility of there not having been help on the spot – there were enough medical workers and ambulances around at the time.

Soon the secret was revealed, and it was a sad secret. Akopyan had never been trapped under rubble, but he was seriously ill and he had been persuaded by his sister to seek treatment in a 'good' hospital in the capital of Armenia. This was the reason for his invented story. The sensational survival had never taken place.

However, if my colleagues wanted an unbelievable story so badly then they could have told, for example, how the army was left to guard a new thousand-bed hospital complex with a collapsed wing and waved through cars which were taking away equipment, linen and medicines from it under the very eyes of the astonished medical staff. 'You'll get replacements,' said the leader of the marauding gang. Isn't that also a sensational story?

Late that evening I was walking along a narrow street in the centre of town, where all the houses were still standing, looking for someone known as the Rescuer. I did not know his address or his surname, only that he came from Moscow and had dragged six live people and forty bodies from under the rubble without the assistance of dogs or heat-seeking equipment.

A little girl came towards me and I asked her where Andrei lived.

'Andrei Terentev? He left this morning. There were no more people where he was working.'

'Did anyone see him off?'

'The whole street – those who were left alive.'

Those who are alive should remember those who came to help – the Russians, British, Georgians, Germans, Lithuanians, French, Ukrainians, Italians, Estonians, Israelis, Moldavians, Norwegians . . . the whole international brigade of clear conscience, goodwill and sympathy.

I returned to Erevan by night and in the morning, at breakfast, I found Sakharov, Galya Starovoitova and Leonid Batkin surrounded by young people, who were all excited. Something important had happened while I was away.

While I had been in Leninakan, Starovoitova and Batkin had visited the top secret location where Ashot Manucharyan, one of the six members of the Karabakh Committee still at liberty, was in hiding. I disclose this with the approval of Galya Starovoitova, but forgive me if I do not mention the address.

One of the movement's activists suggested the meeting with Manucharyan to Galya and Batkin, and, when they agreed, rang a telephone number and said merely 'Synchronise your watches. Go.' From that moment a complex mechanism was set in action. Batkin, who did not know any members of the Committee, waited in his hotel room. He was not told whether they would ring or come for him – he just had to stay in his room.

Starovoitova and her escort left the hotel and set off through the city. Eventually they turned into a narrow street and observed that three men were following them. Passing several houses, Galya and her companion turned into an archway and went straight into a lobby. When the three men came into the courtyard, Galya and her companion re-emerged and came face to face with them, at which the three men, pretending they were looking for something, started gazing at the windows. Galya and her escort walked away, but in the next street they were followed once more.

'Those aren't ours either,' said her companion.

Walking through various yards, they came out into another short street with two men stationed on either side.

'Those are our chaps,' said Galya's escort. They slipped again into a passageway, now without their tail, but accompanied by 'their' men, entered a building and went up to the flat of another activist.

Knowing the telephone was bugged, one of the people in the flat went down two floors to an unfrequented summerhouse and gave the signal for a runner to fetch Batkin.

Meanwhile, a man whom they all knew had come into Batkin's room and had himself suggested a meeting with Manucharyan. In accordance with instructions, Batkin refused the offer, suspecting something fishy. The man left, but his appearance disturbed the group.

The runner who had been sent to fetch Batkin had already been given orders not to bring anyone except him. However, when the runner went into the hotel, using Galya Starovoitova's entry card (needed to gain entry into any Soviet hotel) and went to Batkin's room, he found another member of the Karabakh Committee, Rafael Kazaryan, who had come out of hiding, gone to the authorities and given his solemn undertaking that he would not leave the city.

Kazaryan had realised that Batkin was being taken to a secret flat and had wanted to go along with him. But the runner, with great respect to Kazaryan and although he knew that he, as a member of the Committee, was entirely trustworthy, could not disobey his instruction to just bring Batkin. Kazaryan understood and left. A short while later, Batkin and the runner left the hotel and, having checked several times that they were not being followed, arrived at the appointed place.

At that minute Galya Starovoitova and her escort came out of their halfway house and on a quiet street got into a car with its number plates obscured by snow. They started driving round the city, checking they were not being followed; then, certain that it was all clear, they switched to another car, in which they found Batkin. This car drove into a courtyard and stopped. Nobody followed the car into there and nobody left. Then they drove out into another street and round an ancient quarter of the city. At a pre-arranged point, another car was awaiting them which should have given them a sign. Evidently it was being followed, because as soon as they drew alongside and flashed their headlights in recognition, a strange car came racing out of a sidestreet and gave chase to Galya and Batkin. At once the waiting car came out on to the roadway and put itself between the two cars.

Later, having swapped into yet another car and changed places with people sitting in it, they came back virtually to the place where they had started from in the centre of the city. Without further ado they entered a building, went upstairs, rang the bell in a prearranged code and a woman opened the door, although they knew that Ashot was meant to be on his own in the flat. Then they saw two men and another woman.

A man came up to them, 'My dear guests,' he exclaimed. 'Who are you?' he asked Galya. She said nothing. 'You are not Armenian?'

'I'm Russian,' said Starovoitova.

'If you're Russian, you'll understand us. It was not Russians who fired on us at Zvartnots, they helped us in our hour of need. They are our friends. And what are you?' he asked Batkin.

'I am a Jew.'

'Ah, a Jew. Let me kiss you. Brother, I will never send you away. Let us sit down at the table for a few minutes.'

They had to sit down with these nice people, whose flat they had entered by mistake. When they finally got up to leave, the wife of the second man went up to Galya's escort and said: 'I saw you at a meeting. Be careful, my husband is a policeman.' They left the flat and the building.

It turned out that Ashot Manucharyan was in a neighbouring block of flats, where there was food and drink, and work to be done. They had a long talk. Manucharyan told them the details of the arrest of the Karabakh Committee and that he had decided to go underground until better times came along. But it was not to be. The underground life of the members of the Karabakh Committee did not last long.

Observing the same care as described above, they gathered in a secret flat. Evidently, however, somebody was careless and allowed himself to be followed. They were all arrested on 7 January 1989, five days after the Central Committee of the Communist Party of the Soviet Union, the Supreme Soviet and the Council of Ministers of the USSR had appointed Arkady Volsky to head a special Government committee for Karabakh, extricating Nagorny Karabakh from the political and economic control of Azerbaijan.

To begin with they were held in custody for thirty days, then they were sent to an interrogation and detention centre, where they were not allowed newspapers or tobacco, and criminals lowered cigarettes down to them on string, after which their windows were boarded up. Then they were transfered to prison in Moscow, to the Matrosskaya and the Butyrka.

One spring day at dawn on the roof of a house opposite the Butyrki prison a man stood an instrument case and the quiet of a Moscow morning was filled with the sound of a familiar Armenian horn melody. . . .

Chronology

1988

7 DEC., 11.41: Earthquake, registering more than force 10 at its epicentre, 25 km south-east of Leninakan. Later estimated to be equivalent to 10 of the atom bombs dropped on Hiroshima. 12.20: News of the earthquake received in Moscow at the Ministry of Health. 16.30: First medical teams ready to fly down from Moscow. Gorbachev sends a telegram from New York. Nearest surviving hospitals fill up with wounded.

8 DEC.: First troops arrive in Spitak. During the night 1,500 wounded evacuated by air. Government commission headed by Prime Minister Ryzhkov arrives in Erevan from Moscow and visits disaster areas. In New York, Soviet Foreign Minister Shevardnadze announces that Gorbachev is going to cut short his visit and return to the USSR.

9 DEC.: It is estimated that the number of people in the area affected by the earthquake is about 700,000. Leninakan is four-fifths destroyed; every hospital, polyclinic and maternity home has gone. All 11,000 blocks of flats are damaged or destroyed.

10 DEC.: A national day of mourning is announced throughout the Soviet Union. 40 countries have set up disaster funds for the victims. Gorbachev arrives to visit the disaster areas. He attacks the Karabakh Committee for 'seizing the initiative' in the organization of rescue work. It is estimated that it will cost 5 billion roubles to rebuild earthquake damage.

11 DEC.: Gorbachev flies back to Moscow. The Karabakh issue arises at the press conference before he leaves, and he attacks the movement again. Armand Hammer arrives in Erevan with a cheque for $1 million and a Boeing full of medical equipment.

12 DEC.: During the night a Yugoslavian transport plane carrying aid crashes on approach to Erevan, killing its 7-man crew. 18,500 have now been brought out of the ruins, 5,400 of them alive. 53 nations are now known to have joined in the relief effort. Evacuation of the population from the earthquake zone continues at the rate of 2,000 a day. A further 70,000 need to be evacuated. 500 railway carriages have been sent from the Federal Republic of Germany to accommodate people; dozens of prefabricated houses have arrived from England and Italy; Austria has offered to build a factory to manufacture prefabs in Armenia: 923 foreign rescue workers are on the disaster scene with 216 specially trained dogs. Hundreds of flights have arrived with aid and 1,300–1,400 railways goods trucks a day. More than 5,000 medical workers are now in the disaster area. There is still a dearth of tents and heating especially in the villages near Spitak.

13 DEC.: Doctors for the World, a French organization, arrives in a Boeing 737 with 22 surgeons, anaesthetics and 10 tons of medical supplies, equipment and clothing worth 2 million francs.

14 DEC.: The death toll has risen to 21,775. The situation in a number of districts in Azerbaijan and Armenia remains tense. 150 have been charged with looting from the disaster area. A total of 8 million roubles in cash has been found in the ruins. More than 130,000 Azerbaijani refugees have arrived in Azerbaijan from Armenia.

15 DEC.: The Central Committee of the Communist Party of the USSR allocates 50 million roubles in aid of earthquake victims from Party funds. The first mobile washhouse facilities arrive in Leninakan. Demolition has now begun in areas where all victims have been removed from the rubble. 38,000 have now been evacuated from the disaster area. Foreign aid workers now total 1,500. Ryzhkov criticises poor reception facilities for them (e.g. lack of interpreters). The railway line from Erevan to Moscow is reopened. In Baku 4,749 firearms have been handed in or confiscated. Entry to the city is still restricted.

16 DEC.: The earthquake death toll has mounted to 23,286. At

Zvartnots airport planes are still arriving from Sweden, Syria, Bulgaria, Czechoslovakia, France and the USA.

17 DEC.: Survivors dragged from the ruins total 15,300. Death toll now 23,390. 58 villages are now known to have been destroyed. Over 6 million square feet of living space have been lost in the disaster, as well as more than 6,000 hospital beds and schools for over 100,000 children. A curfew has been imposed in Erevan.

18 DEC.: A total of 70,000 people have now been evacuated from the earthquake area, more than half of them to Soviet republics outside Armenia.

19 DEC.: 514,000 are officially pronounced homeless. 300 tons of food are arriving in the republic every day. Ryzhkov meets Mother Theresa of Calcutta, who is sending nurses to help in the earthquake disaster area. A daily search bulletin is being printed in Armenian and Russian with the photographs, names and addresses of over 100,000 persons for the benefit of friends and relations searching for each other.

20 DEC.: The Government commission headed by Ryzhkov flies back to Moscow from Erevan. To date Armenia has received 1·7 million roubles' worth of food supplies and 4.2 million roubles' worth of other goods.

21 DEC.: Ration ticket system introduced for food distribution in Leninakan. British Government has given £5 million, including 10 plane-loads of aid. In addition, the disaster fund raised by voluntary donations in Britain stands at £7·9 million.

22 DEC.: 77,767 Soviet firms have raised 141 million roubles by donating proceeds of one voluntary working day to the earthquake victims. A total of 22,000 weapons have been handed in in Armenia and Azerbaijan during the amnesty.

23 DEC.: 1,500 tremors have been recorded at the earthquake epicentre since the earthquake struck on 7 Dec.

24 DEC.: Soviet Council of Ministers decides to repair and rebuild

'4 million square metres of private housing, 63 million square metres of school buildings, more than 15 million square metres of pre-school accommodation, hospitals with 4,820 beds and poly-clinic dispensaries capable of dealing with 8,300 visits per session, all within the next two years ... 136 production facilities have lost production capacity of the order of 1,250 million roubles a year ... 150 villages have been wholly or partly destroyed and with them 35,000 inidividual houses ... The current global estimate of the resources needed to rebuild the earthquake zone is between 6–6·5 million roubles, of which 2–2·5 million will be required in 1989.'

25 DEC.: The son and grandson of the President of the USA, George Bush, visit Spitak and Erevan, bringing 40 tons of aid. They are received by Vazgen I.

27 DEC.: Disaster fund now totals 780 million roubles from all sources. The Leninakan bread factory and the telephone system partly reopen.

28 DEC.: Final death toll 24,817.

1989

MAY: A strike centred on Stepanakert starts and continues until September.

JUNE: Clashes between Georgians and Azerbaijanis reported.

JULY: Azerbaijanis killed in Nagorny Karabakh.

AUGUST: Pogrom on Armenians in Baku by Azerbaijanis. People still living in tents in the earthquake disaster area. Much of the foreign aid is reported to have disappeared. In Leninakan the Russian federation which is responsible for 60% of the rebuilding in the city has not completed a single house. An Italian firm has built 250 houses in Spitak. 4,000 troops are stationed in Nagorny Karabakh, which is paralysed by intercommunal fighting, sabotage, strikes and drought. An attempt to set up an 'alternative government in Nagorny Karabakh' is reported. A general strike is called by Azerbaijanis for some time in September.

Soviet Earthquake Scale

The Soviet method of measuring the strength of an earthquake differs from the internationally familiar Richter Scale (source: *Soviet Encyclopedia*):

Grade	Type	Short description
1	Unnoticeable	Only registered on seismic equipment.
2	Very weak	Noticed by certain people in very quiet circumstances.
3	Weak	Only noticed by some people.
4	Measurable	Noticed because of light trembling of objects or window-panes, creaking of doors and walls, etc.
5	Quite strong	General shaking of buildings and furniture, cracking of window-panes and plasterwork. Wakes sleepers.
6	Strong	Felt by everybody. Pictures and walls, bits of stucco fall off. Slight damage to buildings.
7	Very strong	Cracks in the walls of stone built houses. Antiseismic and wooden buildings stay intact.
8	Destructive	Cracks in steep slopes and damp earth. Statues move or fall off their plinths. Houses are severely damaged.
9	Devastating	Severe damage and destruction of stone built houses.
10	Annihilating	Great cracks in the earth. Landslides and avalanches.
11	Catastrophe	Wide cracks in the earth. Many landslides and avalanches. Stone built houses completely destroyed.
12	Severe catastrophe	Exceptional changes in the topography. Many fissures, landslides and avalanches. Birth of waterfalls, springs in lakes, changes in river beds. No construction can withstand it.

Approximate correspondence between magnitude and scale depending on the depth of the centre of the earthquake:

km	magnitude			
	5	6	7	8
10	7	8–9	10	11–12	
20	6	7–8	9	10–11	Io
40	5	6–7	8	9–10	Scale

Io = intensity at epicentre